M000084096

THE BUSINESS
OF COURSES

THE BUSINESS OF COURSES

Abe Crystal, Ph.D.

MIRASEE PRESS

5750 Avenue Notre Dame de Grace
Montreal, Quebec
H4A 1M4, Canada
www.mirasee.com

Copyright © 2021 by Abe Crystal

Paperback ISBN: 978-1-7373742-0-6
Hardback ISBN: 978-1-7373742-1-3
E-book ISBN: 978-1-7373742-2-0

1 3 5 7 9 10 8 6 4 2

CONTENTS

THE EXPERT AND
THE ELEPHANT

AN OLD PARABLE tells of a group of men who learned that a strange creature called an "elephant" had been brought to their town. None of them knew its shape or form, so they sought it out—but it was under heavy guard, so they could only approach it in the dead of night. Fearful to light a fire and alert the guards, they gingerly reached out their hands to learn about this strange creature. The first person, whose hands landed on the trunk, exclaimed that the elephant is long and thick, like a snake. The second, whose hand reached the elephant's ear, described the elephant as being akin to a banana leaf. And the last, who felt the elephant's tail, described it as a rope.

This parable warns us of the dangers of extrapolating from our limited experience and perspective to imagine that we understand the totality of whatever it is that we might encounter—and though the tale is thousands of years old, it applies just as well to the present-day world of online courses.

I've worked in this industry for the past decade, and over that time I've seen experts come and go, each certain that they've found the "one true way" to build and sell online courses. Like the men in the parable, they had direct personal experience supporting the truth that they proclaimed. And like the men in the parable, they weren't even aware of the breadth and nuance of this rich industry that escaped their perception. Yet they succeed because, as the saying goes, in the land of the blind the one-eyed man is king.

Thankfully, aspiring course entrepreneurs don't have to settle for so-called experts who insist that elephants are like snakes, or banana leaves, or ropes. There are real experts in this industry, who have devoted a decade or more to deeply understanding all the different facets and permutations of the online course industry. As you might expect from real, conscientious experts, they tend to be less bombastic than their less savvy peers. They shy away from hype and puffery, and focus on the hard work of helping birth more courses into the world. They trust that their work and expertise will speak for themselves.

The list of these real experts is short, and Abe Crystal sits at the top of it. For more than a decade, he's developed tools and technology to support experts in building online courses that make a real difference for their businesses, and their students. He's seen (and studied!) the full range of ways in which an online course can integrate into a business, and then be executed to create great results for all involved. I've had the privilege of calling Abe a colleague and friend over the years. We share a love for pushing the envelope in the world of online courses, and whenever my team and I want to build something that has a chance at really breaking the mold, Abe is the first person I call. That's why I was so excited that he wrote this book.

There has never been a better time to create an online course. Over the last couple of years, online courses have finally spilled into the mainstream—thanks to the efforts of industry juggernauts like MasterClass, Udemy, and LinkedIn Learning. The broader world is getting used to meetings over Zoom, and highly credible experts are creating their own online course offerings. And that was all true before a global pandemic forced us all to do everything from home, multiplying again the demand for online courses! But finding the right formula for an online course that will work for you and your business takes real insight—the sort that you'll find in this book.

—Danny Iny, Founder and CEO of Mirasee
Author of *Teach Your Gift*, *Effortless*, and *Online Courses*
May 2021 | Montreal, Canada

INTRODUCTION

YOU'VE PROBABLY HEARD that you must *spend money* to *make money*. There's some truth to that old saying. For example, to grow your business with ads, you spend money upfront, then get the revenue later. Or you might spend money shooting pro-quality videos for a new course, expecting the investment to pay off with increased sales and happier clients. Have you considered, though, that in many cases you may instead need to *invest time* to *save time*?

If you feel like you're always working to get the next client, and then dealing with a full calendar serving the clients you bring in, it may be time to take a step back. Ask yourself, *How can I invest time now to save time and free up my schedule in the future?* For many coaches, consultants, and practitioners, reflecting on that question leads to the world of online courses. By delivering courses to your clients, you can serve them more effectively, help them achieve more significant transformations, and better leverage your own

1

limited time. That's what this book is all about: using online courses in your business.

Speaking of time, I know yours is valuable — and you're dealing with a deluge of interesting opportunities and content (I certainly am!). So to respect your time, let me be clear upfront about who this book for and how it can help. Then if you don't find yourself nodding along, you won't need to keep reading.

WHOM IS THIS BOOK FOR?

This book is for experts who love teaching and helping people. You may be a coach, consultant, speaker, trainer, therapist, or other practitioner. You may currently offer services to clients, teach workshops (online or in-person), give keynotes, coach individuals or groups, work with companies on customized consulting engagements, and so on. And you've likely heard some of the hype about offering online courses, but you aren't sure how to make courses work for you.

In particular, you've probably heard some of these ideas about online courses:

- Courses are the key to "passive income" — to earning revenue without directly trading hours for dollars, as you do in coaching.
- Courses empower you to earn far more money than selling services.
- Courses are the key to distinguishing yourself as an authority in your space.

You may even have experimented with offering your own online courses, and hope to do more with them. Alternatively, the very idea of setting up your own course may have seemed so complex or intimidating that you've hesitated even to get started. Wherever you are now, this book will help guide you to understanding the *business* of courses — how you can use courses to better serve your clients, grow your revenue, and make the best use of your precious time.

THE POWER OF ONLINE COURSES

This book is my attempt to cut through some unfortunate hype and misconceptions that have plagued the online teaching and coaching industry. I'll debunk those dated ideas, and then guide you through more effective ways to use courses in your business. This is a critical topic, because online courses have never been more important — for both you and your clients. There are four key reasons you should invest your time and focus in making online courses part of your offerings.

1. Courses establish you as an authoritative, trustworthy expert.

As you help people solve problems, they come to trust you as an "expert." At the same time, there's no need to get too hung up on the word "expert." What matters is that you're able to help people solve a problem, or improve their lives in some way. Providing a course is a powerful way to establish the value you provide to your clients. Your course can cut through the noise of a million blogs and YouTube videos, giving participants a clear path to follow. That sense of direction can come as an enormous relief. You synthesize, simplify, and help people make progress. That earns trust.

2. Courses inspire your followers to action.

In the internet age, there's never a shortage of information. Information alone is useful, but it's only one piece of the puzzle. This problem is older than the internet. How many self-help books are purchased with the best of intentions, then abandoned on a bookshelf or nightstand? What people are hungry for now is not just raw information, but *inspiration*. A great course inspires people to dig deep, to stay focused, and to *implement* the information you provide.

People love to be motivated and inspired, but that's just the beginning. Motivation leads to taking action and getting results. And if you help someone solve a problem, they are likely to share their progress. This could take the form of social media buzz, testimonials, and just good, old-fashioned word of mouth. Your clients become raving fans, and you begin getting more inquiries, more course sign-ups, more Discovery calls for coaching packages, and so on.

3. Courses deepen your relationship with potential clients.

It's one thing to give someone 10 general tips on mountain climbing. It's quite another to walk someone step by step through choosing the best path up a tricky ascent, preparing for the trip, and then listening to how their progress is going along the way. That's one key difference between information and education — between a blog post or article and a well-designed course. In a course, you can see how your learners are progressing, you can give feedback, and you can provide accountability. Information (blog posts, videos, podcasts, etc.) can entertain and inform, but rarely generates any real commitment or a meaningful relationship. When someone signs up for your course, they're making a much more meaningful commitment and so are much more likely to achieve meaningful results. That's the start of a real — and likely long-lasting — relationship, which can lead to ongoing work over time.

4. Courses make a positive impact on the world.

Much of this book focuses on monetization: helping you use courses to get more clients and grow your revenue. That's critical to have a healthy, sustainable business and lifestyle. Yet money isn't what seems to drive most people who ask me questions about online courses or who use the online course platform Ruzuku. They want to see their work *matter*. That's ultimately why courses are so valuable: Helping your clients get results transforms their lives, and that transformation ripples out into the larger world. That's what our work is about at the end of the day: the impact of your gifts on people you care about. You light up when you're solving problems you want to address in the world. Whether your mission is to help people cope with stress in uncertain times, unleash their dormant creativity, or connect more deeply with their kids, seeing your clients make progress is far more meaningful than any dollar amount of revenue.

WHO AM I TO TELL YOU ABOUT ONLINE COURSES?

You may be wondering why you should trust my point of view regarding online courses. I hope you'll find my arguments in the book persuasive, and you should know I've come to these views not through armchair research, but through years of hard-won experience. I co-founded Ruzuku, an online course platform whose mission is to make it ridiculously easy to create, sell, and teach online courses and establish learning communities. And when I started Ruzuku, I had a much more idealistic and naive view of how the business side of courses would work. (See ruzuku.com for details on what we offer).

I came from an academic research background, with a Ph.D. in human-computer interaction. My dissertation research focused on social learning in hybrid and online environments, and I thought the big problem to solve was to create a platform that made it easy for students to learn and collaborate online. Turns out, that's important, but it doesn't help anyone sell any courses! Over the years of experimenting with our own marketing, and talking to thousands of individual course creators, I gradually learned more and more about what it takes to have a successful course *business* — not just a good learning experience. This book is my attempt to distill those lessons learned. I hope it will help you avoid many of the mistakes I made myself! And I'd love to hear your thoughts and questions; my direct email is abe@ruzuku.com, and I'd be glad to connect anytime.

PART I

THE UNTAPPED OPPORTUNITY IN ONLINE COURSES

CHAPTER 1

THE PROMISE & PERIL OF TAKING YOUR WORK ONLINE

IT WASN'T ANY ONE THING that did it. There was no single straw that broke the camel's back. No "eureka" moment. After all, Debra had devoted over two decades to providing training and program development for big-name clients: the Department of Agriculture, IBM, Choice Hotels, the Federal Trade Commission, the American Cancer Association, the University of North Carolina, the National Center for Food Safety and Technology, and many more.

To say she's prolific is more than a bit of an understatement. Debra developed and implemented projects ranging from a business writing series that earned top ratings, to a train-the-trainer curriculum involving more than 1,000 Job Corps students. She designed a customized six-week employee performance training program that helped clients avoid layoffs and shutdowns. And she rolled out a career transition program that her client implemented nationally. She worked incredibly hard to serve her clients and make a positive impact on their cultures, performance, and outcomes. I'm guessing you may see some of yourself and your work in Debra's story. You may also empathize with what happened next.

At some point, a few years back, Debra realized she was maxed out. She'd found herself running between 100 and 130 seminars on the road, every single year. On top of that, she had clients begging her for extra coaching options. Eventually, she realized she couldn't just keep pushing the same brutal schedule month after month and burning herself out in the process. She needed a better, more scalable way to serve her clients with additional coaching programs and courses. She needed to take her work online.

Over the past several years, that's exactly what she's done — with remarkable results. She started with just a single online course. That's how I got to know Debra, in fact; she was beginning to create courses on Ruzuku, the online course platform I co-founded. Since that first course, she's added many more, and built out an entire platform with multiple offerings and collaborators. She's thoughtfully integrated content and course materials from professional providers to speed up her work and launch courses rapidly. As a result, she's been able to serve hundreds of clients and earn tens of thousands of dollars in revenue. Most importantly, she's shifted her work from "crazy and burnout-prone" to "rewarding and sustainable." If you're reading this, you're likely hoping to do the same. And you're not alone.

Debra is part of a wave that's been gathering speed and force over the past several years. Thousands of other experts like her — authors, coaches, consultants, speakers, trainers — are taking their work online. They're creating and facilitating online courses and coaching programs, enabling them to serve more people, free up their time, and scale up new sources of income. As we entered 2020, this shift was already well underway. Then the global pandemic struck.

THE RACE TO MOVE ONLINE

On April 1, 2020, I opened my web browser to start my regular checkup on Ruzuku's monthly hosting costs — the money we pay to the "under the hood" providers, such as Amazon Web Services, who help Ruzuku's infrastructure run smoothly. I wish I had a picture of that moment. I must have looked like a cartoon character, with my hair standing on end and smoke wisps drifting out of my ears. Our hosting bills, across several different online infrastructure providers, were up anywhere from 200% to over 2,200%. *What was going on?!*

In mid-March, lockdown and stay-at-home orders took effect around the globe. Hundreds of millions of people turned to the internet to work, stay in touch with family, play video games, and learn. Sign-ups for online courses skyrocketed. And usage followed, including watching videos, downloading files, and participating in live webinars — all features that Ruzuku offers to our customers, in an easy-to-understand "unlimited" plan. And boy were they putting that "unlimited" pricing to the test! I'd never seen usage like this before, and our team had to scramble to come up with solutions to deliver content at a level we'd never envisioned.

The growth of online courses during the COVID pandemic came as a surprise. Yet when viewed in a larger context, the growth wasn't actually new. Rather, we were seeing an acceleration of a trend that's been building for years. That's why it's important to understand a critical point: You haven't missed the boat. If you've heard of the benefits of online courses in the past, you might feel as if it's too late, that you should have launched your course five years ago, and now the gold rush has passed you by.

But nothing could be further from the truth. Over the past few years, there's been steady growth in how many students are signing up, and how much revenue course creators are earning on the Ruzuku platform. So while it would have been nice if you'd jumped into online courses five years ago, the opportunity to start today is bigger than ever before.

In other words, this is the best time in history to launch your own course. But it's also the easiest time to get pulled into the (legitimate) excitement with disastrous results. The swirl of ideas and strategies available online can lead you to deploy courses in a way that fails to serve you or your customers well. Because online courses are still new and exciting for many experts, it's easy to be drawn to heavily hyped strategies for launching and selling courses. Unfortunately, these strategies can frequently lead you down exactly the wrong path.

GETTING BEYOND THE HYPE

As more people have begun to understand the potential of online courses, a whole cottage industry has sprung up with advice and recommendations. You can now find countless blogs, YouTube videos, and podcasts promising that "you too can be successful with online courses!" Some of these blueprints are even helpful, but they typically only address a specific market segment. Usually, the marketing experts who publish the "blueprint to online course success!" have hands-on experience in a specific market segment. Their experience in that particular segment shapes their guidance on how to create and sell online courses. For example, someone who has had success selling their own premium course on how to run Facebook ads might turn around and offer advice on selling your own course. Their experience, though, is limited to their market subniche — not business as a whole, not even marketing more broadly, but Facebook ads in particular. This narrow focus can lead them to give well-meaning advice that's inapplicable in other contexts.

In this book, I'll do my best to give you a different, and broader, perspective. As the CEO of the online course platform Ruzuku, I've watched this market closely for nearly a decade. I've had a unique vantage point to observe the entire market for online courses, not just one particular subniche. Course creators have launched tens of thousands of online courses on our platform, serving over half a million students. And I've had the opportunity to speak, chat, and email with hundreds of these passionate experts. These conversations have helped me to see the whole landscape and understand what's happening with an array of different courses in different markets and niches. So what I'll share with you in the coming chapters is different than what you might hear from a "blueprint for course-building success" in that blog post or YouTube video you stumbled across. These strategies aren't based on just one opportunity, but on my research into what *all* the opportunities are — all the ways courses can fit into your business and help you better serve your clients.

It's also important to understand that the market for online courses has been changing rapidly since 2012. That's the year the *New York Times* proclaimed "The Year of the MOOC" (referring to Massive Open Online Courses run by leading universities, such as MIT's EdX initiative). The publicity opened many people's eyes to the possibilities of online courses. In the past, if someone thought, "Where can I take a course?" their mental answer was likely to be "at the local college, or at a workshop or retreat." Now their answer is much more likely to be "online." Recent years have also seen a rapid evolution and refinement of online courses offered by individual experts, entrepreneurs, and small businesses. Online courses have started to become a mainstream phenomenon. This means a far bigger market, but also higher customer expectations. And as awareness of courses has grown, so has confusion. Now that there are thousands of places to potentially learn online, many potential customers aren't sure where to start.

Even though online courses have been growing at a remarkable clip for nearly a decade, many people are approaching course creation with expectations and strategies that are badly out of date. To be successful with courses today, you can't just post some content online and hope for the best. You'll need to be thoughtful and strategic. One idea in particular to avoid fixating on is the "big" course. This approach says that you should put all your best ideas into one "be-all-and-end-all" course and focus all your efforts on selling this one course. For most independent experts I work with, this just isn't the best approach. To learn why, we need to turn back the clock to a classic 1980s movie.

"IF YOU BUILD IT, THEY WILL COME"

In the hit Kevin Costner film *Field of Dreams*, a ghostly voice inspires the protagonist to build a baseball field, by whispering:

"If you build it, he will come."

And it works, attracting the ghosts of superstar players past. It makes for a fun movie, especially if you're a baseball fan. But it's a fantasy. Yet somehow, the same wishful sentiment seems to be driving much of the activity I see around real online course development. You know you're succumbing to the *Field of Dreams* fallacy if you're excited about setting up your course and creating lots of in-depth content, but you don't have any kind of strategy for getting customers and growing sustainable revenue. Reflect on whether that captures the approach you've taken to course-building in the past, or that you're considering taking in the future.

The truth is this: Courses are an amazing tool, but not a silver bullet. You can build it and *not* have anyone come. That's why I want to help you think about how to use courses in a new — and vastly more effective — way.

WHY COURSES AREN'T A SILVER BULLET

There are three main reasons why courses aren't a silver bullet to grow your business.

First, just creating a course doesn't mean you'll make any sales. To get consistent sales, you'll need to create the right course for the right people — a course that fits with what your intended client wants and is willing to pay for. Crucially, you also need access to those people (what marketers call "lead generation") and a marketing process that invites them to sign up ("conversion").

Second, even if you have some people interested in your course, you may hit a revenue plateau quickly. For example, if you have 1,000 people on your email list, and 2% of them purchase a course offer from you, that's 20 sales. At $200 per course, that's $4,000. Not bad, but are you going to live on that for a year? For most early-stage businesses, courses need to go hand in hand with services such as coaching and consulting to generate a full-time income.

Finally, the third big reason, the idea that motivates many people to create an online course — earning "passive income" — is largely a myth. Most successful courses require both active marketing efforts *and* active facilitation, support or coaching during the course experience. They're far from passive.

In combination, these three factors contribute to the frustration many coaches and experts feel when they dip their toes into the course-building waters. They start out with enormous enthusiasm, believing that courses can become the driver of their business, and expecting a healthy dose of passive income. But a more common result is to put a lot of effort into content creation, get modest sales, and hit a low plateau for revenue. They're left feeling disenchanted and wondering why that "blueprint to build a money-making online course" didn't work like they expected.

FROM HOPE TO STRATEGY

Well, that all sounds rather disheartening. So why on earth do I run an online course platform? Why do I vigorously encourage people to integrate courses into their business, if the results are so disappointing? It's because courses *can* be genuinely transformative for both you and your clients. But that only happens if you pursue a strategy for using courses that leads to far better results than the *Field of Dreams* approach. The strategy I outline in this book is the strategy I would use to implement courses myself, if I were starting a consulting or service business today. I call it the "Customer Learning Journey Model," and it's the path to using courses to grow every aspect of your business. In the next chapter, we'll dig into this model and discover how it can help you use courses to better serve your clients, grow your business, and leverage your time. You'll learn how you — like Debra — can capitalize on the huge momentum in the online course market.

CHAPTER 2
YOUR CUSTOMER LEARNING JOURNEY

I'VE SENT HUNDREDS OF EMAILS to our community of online course creators, sharing information and inspiration about how to achieve success with courses. Can you guess the subject line of the single email that got the most engagement and response? Here it is:

```
Subject: Course not selling?
```

Why was that email subject line so compelling? I believe it's because most course creators focus on *creating* a course rather than *selling* it. Then they're disappointed when their hard work fails to trigger a flood of sign-ups and revenue. It took me a long time to learn how common this experience is, and it changed my perspective on how to leverage courses most effectively. Courses aren't a magical silver bullet for your business. Yet thanks to massive marketing hype across the industry, a lot of people seem to think they are. Course creators have a strong desire for their courses to serve as the "be-all and end-all" for their business.

As alluring as that vision might be, it doesn't match reality, at least not in my experience. As we saw in Chapter 1, simply creating an online course doesn't mean your business will take off. So where does that leave you? The misleading model of course creation is to jump in and start building a course, and hope that people will buy it from your website, leading to passive income. This approach almost never works, prompting countless frustrated people to reply to my email about their courses not selling. To get better results, you need to shift your approach entirely. The key to unlocking success with courses is to look at the entire *journey* of how people come to find you, and get interested in working with you, and then how you continue to add value for them over time. This is the foundation of building long-term value creation and a sustainable business, of which courses are a vital part — but far from the only component.

UNDERSTANDING YOUR CUSTOMER LEARNING JOURNEY

You can't *not* have a customer journey: By starting a business or practice, and serving customers, you create a journey. But we often lose sight of our customer's journey as we get busy with the day-to-day details of meeting with clients, responding to emails, or filing our taxes. What's hard — even though it pays off more than anything else — is to take the time to step back and think about the person we're really serving, and what journey they take to come to work with us.

Our customer's journey consists of several stages, and we need to support people at each stage. I'll use a five-phase model throughout the rest of the book to help you find ways to grow your business with online courses, rather than getting frustrated that your "labor of love" course isn't selling. Here's a visual overview of the five phases in the **Customer Learning Journey Model**.

Discovery   Engagement   Revenue   Retention   Referral

Phase 1: Discovery

The journey begins with people discovering you exist. And that in and of itself is a real challenge! So many people could benefit from your work. If you're a coach, numerous people could improve their lives with your coaching. If you're a business consultant who solves specific problems, many businesses could benefit from your expertise. If you're a nutritionist, countless people could have better diets and more energy by working with you. But most of the people who could work with you have no idea who you are, what you do, and how you can help. They need to discover your name or brand and what you stand for, as well as your content, your teaching, and your perspective on the world. Until someone comes across your voice and your work, none of the other phases matter. You simply don't exist for them — yet.

That's why the first phase of your customer's learning journey is Discovery. The Discovery phase is about answering this question: How can the right people find you? To do this, you'll need to develop a deep understanding of whom you seek to serve with your courses and business. For example, my company, Ruzuku, provides an online course platform. We're hardly unique in that offering — there are probably hundreds of course platforms out there that people could choose from. That leads us to ask a more specific question: Who are the specific types of course creators we want to attract, and who could be really successful with Ruzuku? What key questions and concerns do they have?

Ruzuku wants to attract independent course creators who are passionate about interacting with and supporting their students. Often, they're running cohort-based courses (taking a group through the program together on the same schedule). They want to have rich discussion and community in their courses. Fundamentally, they want to create a great learning experience and help their students succeed.

That's our example. How do you determine the "right people" for yourself? A good place to start is by asking: What's worked so far? If you've had private clients, which ones have you most enjoyed working with? What are the common characteristics of those "dream clients"? Or, if you've taught live workshops, who were your most engaged participants? Answering these questions will help you design the Discovery phase of your customer's learning journey, which we'll cover in depth in Chapter 3.

Phase 2: Engagement

It's great to have people hear about you and discover you — whether via a friend, a post on social media, a podcast, an ad, or other channels — but that doesn't mean they are immediately ready to buy something from you. They hardly know you at this point! Prospective clients need to reach a certain level of comfort and rapport before they will invest in one of your paid offerings. Establishing this comfort level begins with the deep understanding you're developing as you design your Discovery phase — whom you're serving, and what key questions and concerns they have. Building on the answers to those questions, you'll then need to identify what expertise your prospects are seeking — and how you can demonstrate that your expertise is specifically relevant to them.

In short, you need to *engage* people who have discovered you. You'll do so by addressing this question: How can people come to know, like, and trust you so that they feel comfortable investing in your paid offerings? In particular, what ideas and techniques should you demonstrate and make tangible so potential customers can see that you know what you're talking about?

Before I focused my work on the world of online courses, I consulted in the field known as "user experience." This specialty focuses on making websites and digital products better-designed and easier for people to use. To offer consulting services in this area, I first needed to get people to discover me. I did this by giving talks, writing articles, hosting webinars, attending networking events, and so on.

Once people heard about me, they then needed to get to know me and my expertise better. So, if I were designing the Engagement phase of this customer learning journey today, I might create a free mini-course on "Five Keys to Get Return on Investment from Your Usability Testing." This course would help companies that might want to hire me get to know my expertise and approach better. While the training itself wouldn't deliver any revenue directly, it would lead naturally into the next — and most crucial — phase of the journey: revenue-generating offerings. In Chapter 4, I'll help you design the Engagement phase of your customer's learning to suit your unique expertise and offerings.

Phase 3: Revenue

The next phase may sound obvious: Of course you want to sell things to your customers! But the best revenue strategy isn't so obvious. In particular, it's important not to fixate on just one particular course or offering. Rather than putting all your eggs in one basket, many successful people create a diversified set of offerings. You probably wouldn't put your entire retirement savings in the stock of a single company. Instead, you'd find a mutual fund, or an investment advisor who chooses a diversified set of stocks to reduce risk. In the same way, it's valuable to create an "offering portfolio."

You may look at implementing one or more of these four primary offers, which we'll discuss in more detail in Chapter 5:

1. Flagship course
2. Leveraged coaching
3. Membership community
4. Live events (virtual or in-person)

A **FLAGSHIP COURSE** involves working collaboratively with your participants to help them move toward specific outcomes, with both high-quality content and in-depth support. This is a big project, so it's not necessarily the very first step in your strategy, but it can be one of the highest-impact offers you can create over time.

Private coaching is a straightforward offering — people understand the value of working with you directly and getting personalized attention. Unfortunately, coaching is also inherently unscalable in a private, one-on-one model. That lack of scalability is absolutely fine when you're bootstrapping — you're just trying to get enough clients to pay the bills. As you grow, though, it becomes very limiting. Your calendar is blocked off with call upon call, and you can't handle any more work. At that point, you need to explore how to systematize and **leverage your coaching** approach. You can do this by looking at how a typical client works with you, and then developing assessments, exercises, worksheets, and discussion prompts that clients can complete on their own or as a part of a group.

For **LEVERAGED COACHING**, try reflecting on this question: What can you do that makes a scheduled coaching session with a client at least twice as impactful (because of the work they're doing on their own time and bringing to the session)? Perhaps they're listening to an audio presentation, completing worksheets, and filling out a journal over a period of two weeks before they meet with you. You can get even further leverage with a group model, in which you invite small groups of clients (typically four to eight people) to go through the content and exercises, and participate in small-group calls with you.

A **MEMBERSHIP COMMUNITY** could include ongoing access to content, resources, feedback from you, and online discussions. Whereas flagship courses and coaching programs typically have a defined end, an ongoing membership community provides a way to stay connected to others with common interests. This connection affords a sense of community, mutual support, and peer accountability that many people miss after a program concludes.

LIVE EVENTS offer an intensity of focus that's difficult to achieve otherwise. Both in-person and virtual events have unique benefits and trade-offs. In-person events can be more energizing and provide a greater shift in context and perspective by taking participants away from the routines of everyday life. Virtual events are low-cost and enable you to reach people around the world who couldn't travel to you in person. In either format, you can establish a deeper connection with your community that makes subsequent offers far more likely to resonate.

Finally, you can strategically enhance any of these types of offerings by including **bonuses**. For example, you can package self-study courses with any of your core offerings to augment their value and make them easier to sell. If your leveraged coaching program provides accountability and guidance for small-business owners, you might offer a bonus course on setting and achieving business goals. This bonus both makes the core offer more compelling and helps your clients achieve better results. In Chapter 9, we'll explore whether you should build this type of bonus course yourself or look to acquire "outsourced" course materials.

Phase 4: Retention

Once you do all the hard work of bringing a new customer on board, you'd hope to work with them more than once. The key concept here is the **customer lifetime value**, sometimes abbreviated as CLTV. To grow your CLTV, you'll need to address this question: How do you build a long-term relationship with clients to grow revenue over time? There are two key components to this challenge. The first is the core quality of your offering: making your flagship course, coaching program, or other offering engaging, effective, and valuable for your participants. This is a process: It entails being diligent about going back to customers, getting feedback on their experience with you, and constantly making improvements based on their input.

The second key to the Retention phase of your customer's learning journey is to map out what a valuable, mutually beneficial relationship with your customers could look like over time. Think about the path your clients are on. If they complete an initial course with you, what questions and needs will they have *after* that program? Where will they need support in applying and implementing the ideas in the course? Continue drilling into those open questions, keeping in mind that in most areas of life and work, problems aren't ever fully "solved." Making progress in one area (through a course or coaching program) opens up new questions and opportunities for growth, which in turn leads to new programs and offers.

For example, think about parents of young children who are trying to learn positive discipline techniques. This skill requires behavior change, which is hard! So one single course or coaching program might be insufficient for many people to shift their perspective and day-to-day behavior. A coach in this field might offer a membership program or accountability group with other people experiencing the same challenges, which would help parents continue to make progress. At the same time, this next-level offer increases CLTV as clients "graduate" from the initial course or coaching into the follow-up experience. From a business perspective, having a road map of sequenced offerings can dramatically increase your customer lifetime value. We'll cover how to design this road map for your situation in Chapter 6.

Phase 5: Referral

You've probably heard that the greatest marketing channel is "word of mouth." Enthusiastic referrals from satisfied customers can't be faked, and they're more credible than any marketing campaign you could create. Easy to say, but hard to do — how exactly do you get all those referrals rolling in? Ideally, you'd start a "flywheel" of organic growth.

A "flywheel" in this sense refers to positive feedback loops that build momentum, increasing the payoff of incremental effort. It's hard to get your flywheel started, but once you do, it's incredibly powerful. Here's how it works. You start by getting your first course online and recruiting your first customers. This isn't glamorous. It's often a manual process that relies on personal outreach to your connections. It can take time and effort to get that first group together, and it's unlikely to be a large number of people. But it is a huge step forward to go from zero to one — from never having had a course or any customers to getting up and running.

That first small group of customers isn't worth much on its own. It's rarely enough to make your business sustainable. The opportunity lies in pushing the flywheel forward into the second stage: helping your customers get results, so they're incredibly happy with your course. If your customers become successful, two great things happen. First, people will be raising their hands and asking to work more with you. That means more revenue without having to do any more marketing or find any new customers. Second, they'll be happy to share their great experience with friends, family, and colleagues — or the entire internet via social media! Your customers begin to spread the word. That's how your business and profit begin to grow in a healthy and consistent way. You can further accelerate your flywheel by implementing some smart tactics for getting high-quality referrals. We'll walk through those tactics in Chapter 7.

MEET JANE

The conceptual Customer Learning Journey Model can take you only so far. To really understand how to implement the model, you need a hands-on, concrete example. That's why I'd like you to meet Jane. She's not a real person, but a composite sketch grounded in the experiences of hundreds of real coaches, consultants, authors, and speakers.

Jane is a certified coach, specializing in career coaching, but she also supports people in identifying their broader life goals. Ultimately, she helps clients design a life and career they love. In other words, she's not just about helping someone tune up their resume or find a new job; her sweet spot is helping people craft a fulfilling career and life. Currently, Jane's revenue comes primarily from private coaching clients, although she's also offered a handful of in-person workshops from time to time. These were decently successful, bringing some additional revenue, but not a huge amount. This means she's living in the world of "dollars for hours" — she's only getting paid when her calendar is full of client appointments.

Jane feels fortunate to have an established coaching business, but she'd like more flexibility and income than she has today. These are her goals:

- **BRING IN COACHING CLIENTS MORE CONSISTENTLY.** If it's November, she doesn't want to be stressed out, worrying, "Am I going to have enough clients coming in December and January to pay the bills?" She wants to have confidence that her pipeline of clients will generally be full.

- **DIVERSIFY HER REVENUE SO SHE'S LESS DEPENDENT ON FEAST-OR-FAMINE COACHING.** When coaching is good, it's good — but then her calendar is maxed out. When the phone just isn't ringing with new client inquiries, she feels like she's spinning her wheels, unable to generate revenue with her free time. She wants to be able to earn money even when she's not super-busy with individual coaching clients.

- **START BETTER LEVERAGING HER TIME.** As Jane has gained experience and a strong reputation for her private coaching, she's seen more and more opportunity to expand beyond the "dollars for hours" model. She'd like to find ways to use online programs and group coaching to leverage her expertise.

What should Jane do? And what should you do if you're in a similar situation? I'll give you the overview here, and then in the next few chapters, we'll dig into the tactics and "how-tos" of getting started. There are many strategies that might help Jane move toward her goals, but for now let's focus on three of the most promising approaches.

Strategy 1: A free "lead magnet" mini-course

Jane could start by creating a free mini-course that aligns with the type of clients she wants to attract and work with. To kick-start the Discovery phase of her customer's learning journey, she'd share the mini-course consistently through her personal network and social media with a goal of enrolling at least 10 people per month and booking Discovery calls with at least two or three of those participants. In these Discovery calls, she'd explore people's goals, and then offer to enroll them into a coaching program if it seems like a good fit. This strategy would help her achieve her goal of having a consistent flow of coaching clients.

Strategy 2: A small-group leveraged coaching program

To begin diversifying her revenue and leveraging her time, Jane could develop a group coaching program focused on goal-setting (a common need for her clients). By combining structured content with online discussions and small-group calls, Jane could create an engaging experience for participants, while serving more people than in a private one-on-one engagement. She'd set up this program on an online platform so it's easy for her to manage and for her participants to access. She might start by promoting this program twice a year, with a goal of $5,000 in revenue per promotion (say, 10 sign-ups at $500 per person).

Strategy 3: Themed quarterly workshops

Not all of Jane's prospective clients are immediately ready for the time commitment of a multi-week private or group coaching program. To better serve them, Jane could offer themed quarterly workshops, with follow-up exercises and discussions available in an online program for participants. Not only would the workshops generate revenue directly, but they would also be a great opportunity to invite participants into coaching packages via follow-up calls. Participants who experienced Jane's teaching in the workshops would be primed to consider the value of coaching. This strategy would both diversify revenue and contribute to consistent client enrollments.

One of the challenges with each of these strategies — and particularly with pursuing all three — is the time and expertise needed to build out the relevant materials. To develop the mini-course, for example, Jane might need to research goal-setting concepts, and develop new written materials such as worksheets, discussion questions, and slides. This could be a significant effort, which raises the question of whether she should do this herself or enlist help. We'll come back to this key question in Chapter 9.

But first, we are going to explore each phase of the customer's learning journey in more detail. We'll begin with the first phase, Discovery. What does it take to help people discover you and your work? How can you use courses to make your Discovery phase as effective as possible? Read on to find out!

PART II

HOW TO DESIGN YOUR CUSTOMER LEARNING JOURNEY

CHAPTER 3
DISCOVERY: HELP THE RIGHT PEOPLE FIND YOU

> **Pushing on a string.** Expression: "A strategy that is fundamentally flawed and not capable of solving a chosen problem, even with tremendous effort."
> — Urban Dictionary

MANY EXPERTS, consultants, and coaches become disillusioned with online courses when they've put a lot of effort into creating a course, only to find that it doesn't generate any sales. If you try that strategy, and then try it again — with more effort and determination — and it yields the same disappointing results, you're getting firsthand experience with *pushing on a string*. Anytime you experience that disheartening feeling, it's time to step back, reflect, and then shift your strategy. What do we see when we step back and look at the bigger picture?

The core flaw in this strategy of jumping right into offering a course for sale is that *before* you can offer any kind of course or service, people need to know you exist! (Not only that, but they also need to trust the credibility and value of your work — but we'll return to that issue in Chapter 4.) Creating a paid course doesn't help anyone find you or your offerings. Yet too often, this is what we see in practice: believing, and hoping, in a "build it and they will come" approach. This is where so many expertise-based businesses fail to get off the ground, or to expand beyond a few initial clients. And it's true in every industry. A story that gets told again and again in the world of high tech goes like this: Brilliant engineers invent a super-cool new product or app that does all kinds of neat things. They put up a website and wait for customers to beat down their virtual door. The chirping of crickets ensues. Brilliant engineers give up and go back to punching the clock for a giant tech company, tails between their legs.

In other words, it's hard to get customers, no matter how good your offering, and no matter what industry or niche you're in. Frankly, there's nothing I can tell you that will make getting clients "easy." The only viable approach is to make this challenge one of your core priorities, and to work on it consistently, week in and week out. In addition, you can use the power of online courses to help people discover you and your work. But it's not just about getting *anyone* to discover you — it's about helping the *right* people find you. Think about these questions:

- Whom do you want to reach out to you tomorrow?
- What are the characteristics of the client that you'd be super-excited to hear from?

Now think about the fact that this ideal client — the person you dream of working with — has no idea who you are or how to find you. You need to help that person reach you — as soon as possible! That's exactly what Discovery is all about — taking two key steps that make it dramatically easier for the *right* people to find you. First, create valuable educational content and experiences, and make them available at no charge. Second, spread the word about these free offerings, by making them available via a number of different "distribution channels." Let's take a look at the details of each of these two key steps.

STEP 1: CREATE A COMPELLING FREE OFFER

Several years ago, my company, Ruzuku, was struggling to attract customers. We'd put up a shiny new marketing website that sung the praises of our innovative online course platform. Through partners, blog posts, and sheer hustle we'd managed to bootstrap some traffic to the site, and the graph in Google Analytics was starting to slowly inch upward each month. There was just one problem: Hardly any of those visitors were purchasing our service, or even contacting us with questions. We could keep pushing harder to get more visitors, but our ability to engage those visitors was so low, it wouldn't help very much. All our work seemed pointless.

Eventually, it occurred to me to stop "pushing on a string" and try something different. I realized that many people were curious about online courses, but not ready to purchase a platform right away; they needed to learn more about the process first. In addition, our website was reaching only a tiny fraction of potential course creators. We needed to get our expertise and perspective out to a much broader audience, beyond our own website and blog. I sat down with our team and we started mapping out our first compelling free offer — a mini-course (offered on the Ruzuku platform, naturally!) called "5 Steps to Your Online Course."

We provided this mini-course for free. And since we launched it, it's served over 12,000 eager course creators around the world and become a crucial part of our business. The free training gives people a strong reason to connect with us and opt in to our mailing list, even if they're far from ready to pay for our service. And because this offer is free, we've had success sharing it widely — on social media, with partners who email it to their audience, and via ads. It's grown our audience, built word of mouth, and ultimately brought in many new customers (partly because, as we'll see in the next chapter, it builds trust before people buy from us).

So that's your opportunity as well — to define a compelling free offer (sometimes called your "lead magnet" or "first impression incentive"). You've doubtless encountered this strategy yourself when browsing around online — it's the classic "Hey, enter your email address to download my free e-book on five tips to reduce stress" or "Register for my free webinar on optimizing profitability in your business." There are countless different free offers like these that you *could* provide. The challenge is to create something of value *and* distribute it in places where people can discover it.

This strategy is straightforward, although it'll likely take some trial and error to get it working for you. Designing an effective free offer — one that will pique the interest of your prospective customer and motivate them to sign up — starts with four core questions:

1. Whom are you serving?
2. What are their core needs and questions?
3. What's the first step on the journey to addressing those needs and questions?
4. What specific offering will help people get started with that first step?

Whom Are You Serving?

This is the foundational question that is crucial to keep asking and answering, again and again. It's easy to drift away from a clear focus on whom we're creating our offers *for*. We need to keep asking: Do I have a crystal-clear definition of whom I'm serving? If you're not sure where to start, try filling out the "customer persona" shown on the following page.

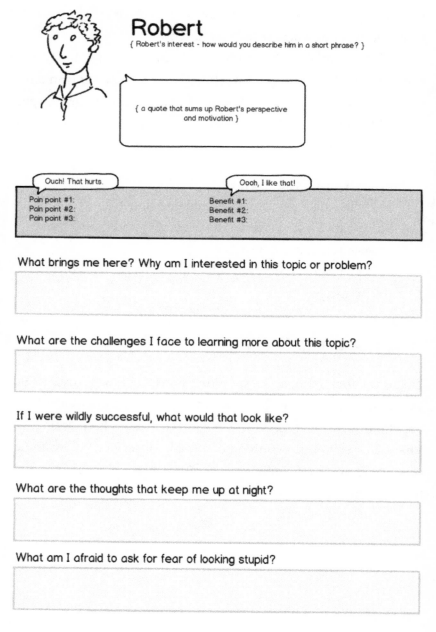

Robert

{ Robert's interest - how would you describe him in a short phrase? }

{ a quote that sums up Robert's perspective and motivation }

Ouch! That hurts.

Pain point #1:
Pain point #2:
Pain point #3:

Oooh, I like that!

Benefit #1:
Benefit #2:
Benefit #3:

What brings me here? Why am I interested in this topic or problem?

What are the challenges I face to learning more about this topic?

If I were wildly successful, what would that look like?

What are the thoughts that keep me up at night?

What am I afraid to ask for fear of looking stupid?

What Are Their Core Needs and Questions?

Once you have a specific client in mind, you can then explore the particular needs and questions of the people you're looking to help. Let's say you're looking to create a lead magnet mini-course that ties in with your work on stress reduction. That's great — but stress is a *big* topic! How could you focus that more sharply? Perhaps you want to focus on helping parents of young children deal with stress. Now we're getting somewhere: You can unpack the needs and questions that those particular customers might have, and use those to inform your lead magnet. If you have an audience on social media or a mailing list or both, surveying people who follow your work about their key needs and questions could also be a great way to inform your choice of lead magnet.

What's the First Step on the Journey to Addressing Those Needs and Questions?

As you begin to design the free offer, it's critical to understand that you're not trying to deliver a big pile of content for free. The goal isn't to give away the farm, or to create a free offer that obviates the need for your paid offer. Rather, it's to help people take one meaningful step toward the outcomes they're interested in so they're excited about working more with you. Take some time to reflect on what a "first step" might look like for your particular customers. In our stress reduction example, the first step might involve examining one's current beliefs about stress and completing a "stress mindset" assessment. A mini-course on these topics would help lay the foundation for further work on understanding and managing stress.

What Specific Offering Will Help People Get Started with That First Step?

There are many types of free offerings you could create. Common ones include free reports, e-books, videos (or a series of videos), audio downloads, and the like. You may even have signed up for some of these yourself!

Now, obviously I'm biased in favor of courses, but I honestly do recommend that you consider a free mini-course as a potential lead magnet. Considering their power and benefits, courses are still underutilized as lead magnets. There are many benefits to courses:

- Courses provide higher perceived value for your customer, as compared to an e-book or other resource. Think about which sounds more powerful: "enter your email address to get my free report on five tips to reduce stress," or "enter your email address to get my free mini-course with step-by-step guidance on how to reduce stress, plus exercises and discussion prompts." A course connotes value and authority — and that's valuable.

- Courses also afford the possibility of structure, support, and interaction. You can easily set up a series of short modules with discussion questions (on a platform such as Ruzuku), which creates a much more in-depth and engaging experience for your customer. This is exactly what we do with our "5 Steps to Your Online Course" mini-course.

- Courses can contain a variety of media and formats to engage your prospective clients. A single mini-course could include text, images, an audio interview, a personal video from you, and PDF handouts that participants can download and print out. This range of formats makes people more likely to engage, take action, and want to work further with you.

Let's make this more concrete by returning to the example of Jane, the coach who helps people design a career path and life they love. As we discussed previously, one of Jane's key goals is to bring in clients more consistently. To do that, she plans to create a free mini-course that will help people discover her and her coaching. The key to making this lead magnet successful is answering each of the four core questions.

Q: Whom is Jane serving?
A: Mid-career, highly educated professionals who feel burned out or unfulfilled. They're in a cycle where they've been doing the same things for a long time, and they aren't used to coping with these feelings of being "stuck."

Q: What are their core needs and questions?
A: Feeling "stuck," but not sure how to get started thinking about different approaches. Nervous about being outside their comfort zone.

Q: What's the first step on the journey to addressing those needs and questions?
A: Self-awareness and identifying the problem — beginning to recognize and grapple with the fact that they are feeling "stuck." Recognizing that there are areas of their life and work that they'd like to change — areas where they feel they're living at "3 out of 10" rather than "10 out of 10."

Q: What specific offering will help people get started with that first step?
With those answers in mind, Jane's mini-course could be something like this:

Discover Hidden Burnout: How to Know When You're "Hitting the Wall" in a Successful Career and Life.

In the course, she would walk people through an assessment of 12 key areas of life and work. This assessment would help them identify some of the symptoms and emotions they might be experiencing. This would help people to determine for themselves: "*Am* I feeling stuck in my life and career?" You can see the logic of this approach: Jane's helping people open up new possibilities for their lives, and she's motivating them to want to solve this newly apparent problem — which could mean working with Jane!

To summarize, creating an effective course for Discovery isn't just about throwing some free content against the wall. It's about finding the approach that will "click" with the right type of customers — the people you want to work with, and who value your expertise. Sometimes this is a mini-course or other content you'll build yourself from scratch. What I frequently hear from people, though, is: "But I don't have time to build out all these free courses myself. I know potential clients would value it, but I'm busy actually working with my current clients!" An important strategic question to consider is if you should build your Discovery courses yourself or look into licensing them from a professional content provider. We'll break down this "build versus buy" decision further in Chapter 9.

STEP 2: EXPERIMENT WITH MAKING YOUR OFFER AVAILABLE IN DIFFERENT PLACES SO PEOPLE CAN DISCOVER IT

Creating a free course won't on its own do much — you need people to *find* the course! The problem is, you won't know where people will find your free lead magnet and sign up for it until you try some different approaches. What I recommend is that you make a list of places to try, and then systematically start testing and tracking your efforts.

But where do you start? Where could people discover your free offering? You'll need to identify possible places where those people "hang out." The good news is there are more potential places than ever for people to discover your work!

To begin, return to your earlier analysis of whom your intended customer is, and what questions and needs they have. Then you can "reverse engineer" where people with those needs and interests are, and where they would discover your free offering. I'll give you a whole set of options to consider shortly, but first let's look at how this might play out for Jane's example: How could she help people discover her free mini-course?

First, Jane might consider social media. LinkedIn seems like the most logical platform to explore, given its professional focus. People might be viewing LinkedIn to check on a former colleague or research a client. While they're on the site, they may browse through their LinkedIn feed to see what's new. If Jane is posting her ideas and free mini-course consistently to LinkedIn, people will have a chance to discover it in time. She could also look at implementing a similar strategy on Facebook.

Another approach is direct outreach. Whom has she talked to, emailed, or had a meeting with in the past year or two? (Her calendar and "Sent" folder are great resources to browse through here.) She'd then start sending brief, personal notes via email to these contacts, introducing her mini-course, inviting them to take it for free, and asking if they know anyone else who'd be interested in it. While this is a relatively slow, manual strategy, it's extremely powerful because direct, personal emails from a real person are much more likely to be read (and acted on!) than a random social media post, or an email newsletter going out to thousands of readers.

Next, Jane could explore communities that fit with her work. Perhaps she's noticed that she frequently gets referrals from HR professionals. Based on that experience, it seems promising to connect with communities of HR practitioners. For example, she could reach out to a local HR association, where she has some contacts, about hosting a webinar for their members. Or, since she knows that mid-career professors are some of her best coaching clients, she could find ways to share her mini-course with universities and academic associations.

It's also important for Jane to track her progress over time to gain insight into which approaches are most fruitful. It's best to start simple with this sort of tracking. She might keep a notebook or spreadsheet, update it each week with the outreach she attempted, and see what the results have been. This table shows some examples.

Channel	Week 1	Week 2
LinkedIn	Posted 3x: tips, and invitation to join free mini-course. Results: 2 comments, 3 shares, 1 sign-up to mini-course.	Posted 3x: questions, and invitation to join free mini-course. Results: 5 comments, 1 share, 4 sign-ups to mini-course.
HR community	Asked Cathy re: offering a free webinar. Result: They are open to it and looking at dates in a month or so.	Started a discussion in the association's online forum re: identifying signs of burnout in employees. Result: 5 people have responded.

FINDING THE RIGHT CHANNELS

Now you've seen how Jane could begin identifying and tracking potential "Discovery channels" (a fancy way of describing the places people hang out, where they could learn about her expertise). You're probably eager at this point to figure out how you could do the same for your courses and business. Following is a more complete list of channels you can test as you work to help more people discover you. Bear in mind that this isn't intended to be an exhaustive list, and you can (and should!) brainstorm alternative ideas that would be worth testing in your specific situation, but there should be plenty of ideas here to get you started!

Social Media

The first category of Discovery channels is social media. Each platform is unique, so you'll need to come up with an approach specific to a particular platform; it's not sufficient to simply post the same content everywhere and hope for the best.

Facebook

Facebook's strength is personal interaction. You can start by posting ideas and sharing interesting content with your personal network. Also consider hosting via Facebook Lives, where you deliver short presentations and take questions. You can also create your own private group that you invite people to join so they can connect with you.

LinkedIn

LinkedIn is more focused on content and updates. You'll need to provide both engaging content and a strong point of view. Engaging content could include essays, tips, and videos that relate to your core teaching and the problems you help clients address. And it's important that you share ideas that you believe in — ideas that reflect your unique point of view. In other words, be yourself! For inspiration, check out the work of John Corcoran, who is a master at building an audience on LinkedIn. Search for his name on that platform and browse through his content (see https://www.linkedin.com/in/corcoran/). In particular, notice how he hosts interviews with interesting guests — this is a creative way to share valuable ideas, and also to reach more people through the guest's audience.

Twitter

Twitter is a fast-paced, global conversation. It can be chaotic at times, but it's also a great place to get your voice heard. You can start by finding interesting people to follow, participating in conversations, and sharing your work when relevant. On Twitter, you'll need to be extremely concise and clear, both because of the platform's short message limits and also because people are scanning quickly through tweets, looking for nuggets of insight.

YouTube

YouTube is all about video. People come to YouTube to find a specific video that will help them with a problem or question, or more generally to be entertained, educated, or inspired. This is the place to share your expertise with teaching videos, bits of motivation, and helpful tips.

Reddit

Reddit is home to thousands upon thousands of niche communities. If you want to geek out on super-fancy headphones or discuss *Game of Thrones*, Reddit has a place for you. Your mission here is to find relevant "subreddits" (specific communities) and participate in discussions, ask interesting questions, and learn the culture of Reddit's unique community.

Personal Connections

Direct email outreach to friends, colleagues, and connections is one of the simplest channels to test and can often yield great results. You can start with an email like the example shown here, customized to your needs.

Subject: Might be of interest?

Hi [NAME],
How have you been? What's new since [we talked at this conference / had a meeting / etc.]?

Thought this might be up your alley — I just put together a new mini-course on [QUESTION/PROBLEM YOUR COURSE ADDRESSES].

Interested in checking it out? I'd love to hear your thoughts!

Let me know and I'll send you a link to hop in (no charge obviously, just interested in your comments).

Best,
[YOUR NAME]

One note about this email format: Though it may seem counter-intuitive, we recommend that you ask people to reply to this email, rather than simply sending them a link directly. The reason is that replying to the message creates more of a sense of connection than simply clicking a link, and it also provides an opportunity for them to ask questions and start a conversation with you.

Associations

Professional associations provide a great opportunity to connect with a specialized group of people. Let's say you teach productivity skills for project managers — professional associations of project managers would be an important channel for you to experiment with. In most cases, you're not looking to sell directly to the association or its members (although some associations could be open to a partnership in which they market your courses in exchange for a share of revenue). Rather, you'll create valuable content that establishes your expertise and helps members discover your work. This could entail writing for the association's blog or newsletter, hosting webinars, or speaking at conferences. These "attention-getting" activities will help you establish yourself as an expert, and make it easier for people to discover your courses.

APPLY IT

Now it's your turn.

First, think through what could serve as your compelling free offer. You might take a sheet of paper, or fire up a document on your computer, and reflect on your answers to the four core questions:

1. Whom are you serving?
2. What are their core needs and questions?
3. What's the first step on the journey to addressing those needs and questions?
4. What specific offering will help people get started with that first step?

Next, brainstorm *where* people might be able to discover your free offer. What are three places you could test? Go through this list, as well as any other ideas you have, and make notes on where you could start sharing your expertise so people can discover you and your work. This is the first step in mapping out your customer's learning journey. In the next chapter, we'll discuss the next phase of the journey: building engagement and trust with prospective customers.

CHAPTER 4

ENGAGEMENT: THE JOURNEY TO TRUST

IN THE LAST CHAPTER we explored one of the biggest challenges you face as an independent course creator: your ideal client — the person you dream of working with — has absolutely no idea who you are or how to find you. You need to make it easy for that person to *discover* you. That's what the first phase of your customer's learning journey is all about.

However, people don't typically segue from "Hey, I just heard of this Abe guy," to "Wow, let me buy his $1,000 course right away!" If you focus on Discovery, but then start throwing expensive offers at people who've just learned about you, you'll likely wind up with a big fat zero in your sales spreadsheet. Not much fun.

There are a few exceptions. If you solve a really pressing problem that demands immediate attention, then your customers are much more likely to purchase your course or service right away. For example, suppose a company that relies heavily on Facebook ads for marketing has had their account suspended by Facebook. They want a solution, as soon as humanly possible. If you can provide that via your service or training, they probably won't hesitate to sign up the moment they find you. They're willing to take the risk that your offering isn't exactly what they need, because even the possibility of a solution is incredibly valuable.

Far, far more commonly, though, you must build trust, rapport, and credibility first. And that takes time. You'll need to answer this question: How can people come to know, like, and trust you enough that they feel comfortable investing in your offerings? The answers to this question will inform the Engagement phase of your customer's learning journey. This phase is about nurturing the relationship — helping people get to know you, learn from you, and recognize your expertise. Let's look at this process in the context of the five-phase learning journey. Think about your prospective customer who comes to your free lead magnet offer (such as your free mini-course) and signs up. What happens next? We don't want that experience to end abruptly!

Instead, you should seek to "nurture" new contacts — educating people at no charge or through low-cost, accessible offers, or both. Free nurture content might include an educational email sequence or community webinars. A low-cost offer might be a $47 workbook that someone purchases between signing up for your free webinar and your $3,000 coaching package. So that's how the Engagement phase fits into your learning journey. Let's dig into the primary strategy for engaging people: providing nurture content.

"NURTURE" CONTENT

There are two reasons why it's especially critical to provide useful and engaging nurture content for people who opt in to your free offer. The first is that there's something special about educating and engaging with people consistently over time. Providing an impressive collection of high-quality and relevant information up front doesn't build as much trust and credibility as educating and sharing over time. We naturally tend to associate consistency and continued performance with reliability and trustworthiness. That's why it's so important that you connect with your prospective clients *multiple* times in the Engagement phase of your customer journey.

To understand the power of repeated exposure, consider a fascinating study conducted by psychologists Richard Moreland and Scott Beach. The researchers arranged for four different women (of similar appearance) to attend a college class a certain number of times throughout the semester, but not to interact with any of the students in the class at all. In other words, they appeared to be people who were just auditing or sitting in on the class lectures. Three of the women attended different numbers of class sessions (5, 10, or 15). One woman did not attend class but posed as a student for a photograph that was converted to a slide. At the end of the semester, the students in the class saw pictures of each of the "auditing" women and rated them on several scales, such as familiarity and physical attractiveness. Despite *never having interacted with these women at all*, the students showed a clear "mere exposure" effect. They evaluated the woman they had seen 15 times as more attractive, familiar, and similar to themselves than the woman they hadn't seen at all.

That's the power of simply being exposed to another person repeatedly — and the same "mere exposure" effect applies to ideas as well. The more you're exposed to a person or idea, the more comfortable you become with her or it. That's why marketers often reference "the rule of seven," meaning that a potential customer needs to see or hear from your brand or your offering seven times before buying. There's no exact science as to this precise number, but the general principle is sound: The more positive interactions people have with you, the better. That's exactly why you should nurture people who discover you so they develop familiarity with an affinity for your work, through repeated "exposure."

A Real-World Example of Nurture Content

Let's take a look at an example of a real lead magnet and nurture sequence from my company, Ruzuku. As I mentioned in Chapter 3, we offer a free mini-course called "5 Steps to Your Online Course." People can find this course on our website and blog and via referrals and join for free.

Once someone signs up, they receive access to five course modules on Ruzuku, including a framework and tips for designing their own online programs. So that's the initial Discovery phase of our customer journey: We provide a valuable free offer, and people find it through online searches, social media, and other channels. The next step is Engagement: Once someone interested in course creation signs up, they'll start receiving our sequence of nurture emails. This is a fairly in-depth nurture email sequence, which continues for around three weeks. To give you a sense of how this sequence looks, here's a sample of the email subject lines and topics:

Subject line	Topic
Welcome to 5 Steps to Your Online Course	Welcome and ask for key challenges
Step 1: Why you should design your course backwards?!	Consumption (come back to the course)
Bonus: A 17-point checklist to help you prepare for your next course launch	Engagement (build continued interest)
Checking in — how is your course coming along?	Nurture
5 tools to help you create your course	Nurture

Overall, this sequence works to keep people engaged, to build trust over a period of time, and to establish Ruzuku as a trustworthy provider if they decide to move forward with building their online course. It's important to understand that it's not just a collection of 15 emails. While any consistent email outreach is better than none, what helps make this sequence effective is that it progresses through a series of phases, as shown on the following page.

We've designed six phases of this nurture sequence. First, we welcome people into the course and email series, and help them feel "at home." We encourage them to get in touch and ask for help — this isn't intended to be purely passive content sequence. In particular, in the welcome I ask for their questions and challenges. Here's how it looks.

Hi Jessica,

I'm so glad you're joining us.

Our mission is to unlock the expertise of passionate, independent experts.

That's where you come in.

We want to help you create and launch online courses, so you can help more people, in a way they can afford — while building your own business.

This 5-step course will challenge you to get started on designing and publishing your own course.

It may not always be easy or comfortable.

But we'll be here to support you along the way.
Reply to this email and tell me what you're struggling with right now.

Even if it's something really small, don't hesitate. I read every single reply.

Then start here: <u>Welcome and getting started with the course</u>.

Cheers,
—Abe

P.S. This course is hosted on <u>Ruzuku</u>, our online learning platform. If you're curious to learn more about Ruzuku's course creation features, <u>hop into our 100% free no-obligation trial</u> and get access to our in-depth tutorial course: <u>Ruzuku 101: Create, Sell and Teach Your Course</u>.

Next, we encourage people to come back to the course — the consumption stage of the nurture sequence. Here's the first email in the consumption stage.

Welcome back!

First things first: If you haven't yet, <u>join our online course and community now</u> to get all the resources and support.

Great. Now we're going to kick you off with something that may be a bit counterintuitive at first. But it really WORKS.

Typically, when we ask people to start thinking about creating an online course or program, they immediately start talking about CONTENT. "I'm going to talk about X, Y, Z…and then we'll have this cool worksheet, and then…"

We'll get there. But not yet. It's too soon.

We need to start with the fundamentals.

Ask yourself: Who is your program for, and how is it going to help make a positive impact on your participants' lives?

To get really concrete about this, we're giving you your first challenge. We want you to think about a sales page for your program, BEFORE you do anything else. This exercise will dramatically clarify your thinking and prepare you to launch your program as soon as you can.

Homework for Step 1: Answer the 6 key sales page questions

1. Whom are you serving? Whom are you not serving?
2. What is the problem? Write down your target audience's problem(s).
3. What is possible? Write down what's possible if your customer's problem is solved.
4. What are the top three emotional/psychological/spiritual benefits you hope to deliver?
5. What are three specific topics you will cover to help people get these benefits?
6. Imagine and write a testimonial from a future student.

Take action: <u>Share your answers to the questions in this activity on Ruzuku ></u>

Best,

—Abe

Co-founder, Ruzuku

P.S. If you feel like you need a little extra support, we save a few 20-minute slots each week to help people going through this program. Reply to this email and we'll find time for a quick call to get you going.

These emails are focused on encouraging people to really dive into the course materials and take action — to go beyond just skimming or being generally curious. What we really want is for them to start using all the ideas and exercises in "5 Steps to Your Online Course." The more they do that, the more value they'll get out of the program, and the more likely they'll be to start moving forward on their own course idea. That's what real "engagement" looks like — people are energized, taking action, and getting value from your free offering. That momentum, in turn, leads to customers: You've built the credibility and trust necessary for someone to invest in your paid offerings.

The next stages in this nurture sequence attempt to provide some different ways for people to engage. We recognize that we can say, "Hey, go check out the course and take action!" only so many times before it becomes numbing. So in the next two stages of the sequence, we first invite people to schedule a free consultation if they have questions or need help. Then we share tips and tools that might be useful to people creating their first online course. The fifth stage represents a bit of a pivot. At this point, we've provided all kinds of useful information and action steps. More information isn't going to help — and could even start to overwhelm people. Instead, we shift into motivation: inspiring people to connect with the reasons and emotions that pull them to want to create a course.

In particular, we've observed that many of our best customers are interested in helping people and making connections — these values are more important to them than earning a lot of money. So in the motivation stage of the nurture sequence, we speak to the power of connection in online courses:

Subject: The shift from "building reach" to "nurturing connection"

Let's talk about how you can build a sustainable, profitable business around your courses.

For now, I'm going to assume that you offer some kind of professional service, such as:

Coaching, consulting, writing, design, outsourcing, and so on.

Your course is the perfect vehicle to engage people and lead them naturally into your service offerings.

It's all part of a paradigm shift in online marketing, from building "massive reach" to nurturing deeper connection.

We can't just copy the old "get traffic, get subscribers, sell products" playbook anymore.

Instead, it's paramount to really build and nurture your community.

The experts who thrive will be the ones who have built these strong community bonds.

And one of the most powerful ways to nurture your community is to educate and inspire.

So building a course is a way of building your community or tribe.

And this is the path to success as we move forward.

Now, this doesn't have to mean you create a huge flagship training and charge hundreds of dollars for it.

You can also deepen relationship with your community through focused, short, free courses.

These "mini-courses" can be powerful sources of leads for your core business — whether that's consulting, coaching, or a specialized service.

The free (or even low-cost) course is the ambassador of your business.

It means that every day, people can be learning from you and deepening their connection with you — without you even being there.

And then the opportunities "pop out." Hey, I need some coaching on X. Hi, I'd love for you to speak at my workshop on Y.

The most powerful way to generate clients online is through word-of-mouth marketing — and courses can generate incredible word of mouth.

Because when someone learns from you, she feels excited and empowered.

She wants to share that feeling with others.

That's how your business grows in a deeply personal and sustainable way.

Just "getting people on your list" isn't enough anymore.

You have to think about what value participants are getting from you, and how you can build a deep connection with each and every learner who spends time with you.

That's what a well-designed course can do.

We'd like to help you get your course idea out of your head, and into the world.

Reply if there's anything I can do to help,

— Abe

P.S. Next time we'll share some tactics for ramping up your revenue from your courses. So stay tuned for those ideas, coming soon.

Finally, we wrap up the sequence by reminding people that they have continued access to the training, that we're here to help them anytime, and that Ruzuku is available when they're ready to create their own online course. So that's the arc of the nurture sequence, from welcoming and engaging people, to sharing tips and motivation, to closing the loop. And to clarify, there's no magic timeframe for an email sequence such as this one — we could have kept going with even more emails, and I've seen examples of email nurture sequences that last a year or even longer! But for our purposes, this length of sequence works well. It's also important to start small, and have at least some nurture, rather than setting yourself an impossible goal and never getting past the starting block.

You're probably not developing a free offer and nurture sequence that's specifically about online courses, so let's also explore an example that might be closer to the coaching, consulting, or teaching you do. Our next example is a nurture sequence from "Go for Your Goals," which is a course in our "Instant Courses" library of professional-designed "done for you" courses. This sequence follows a related but different set of stages, as shown here.

Here's the full list of email subject lines and topics.

Number	Subject	Topic
1	Welcome to "Go for Your Goals"	Welcome and ask for key challenges
2	How are you doing?	Consumption (come back to the course)
3	Special offer (students only)	Invite to Discovery call

4	The value of an outside perspective	Encourage engagement with course + Discovery call
5	Don't skip THIS key step	Encourage engagement with course + Discovery call
6	Last chance for FREE strategy call	Urgency to book call

This sequence works a bit differently because it has a specific goal: to invite people to a free coaching call. On this call, the coach or consultant (that's you!) speaks with the prospective client about their goals, and then offers a paid coaching package, if it's appropriate and seems like a good fit. So this sequence has an explicit focus on inviting people to book a call, and it contains multiple emails with that specific call to action (book a free coaching call). The sequence uses different angles to get people interested in considering that call. For example, email #4 in the sequence emphasizes the importance of getting coaching or outside perspective, as shown here.

SUBJECT: The value of an outside perspective

Hi [FirstName],

Ever have a friend come to you for advice on a sticky problem...

...and to you, the solution is glaringly obvious?

That's the power of an outside perspective.

Whatever your situation is, by definition, you're INSIDE it. (That's why we say we're "in a situation"!)

And it's really hard to get a clear view of anything from inside.

That's why working with a coach, mentor, or outside expert can be so incredibly powerful. A good coach can see things that you cannot, identify opportunities that you're blind to, and help you make the key decisions that will determine your ultimate success or failure.

I want you to have that experience.

So for the next [instructions: indicate how long the offer is good for], you can register for a totally free, one-on-one strategy session with yours truly.

We'll dig into where you want to go, the fastest way to get there, and the action steps you'll need to take along the way. And you'll leave with more clarity and confidence about the path you've chosen.

Sound good? <u>Go here to grab a spot on my calendar.</u>

Talk soon!

What's most important is not the details of each specific email, but that you take the time to create a nurture sequence that will be engaging and interesting for your potential customers.

CUSTOMIZING YOUR CALL TO ACTION

You can take this approach one step further by aligning the invitations in your email sequence with what's best for engaging with your prospective clients. Although holding one-on-one Discovery calls (via phone or videoconference) works well for many coaches and consultants, there are other powerful ways to connect with people. Here are some actions you could invite prospective clients to take:

- Attend a free webinar.
- Join my low-cost self-study course.
- Buy my workbook.

What we generally *don't* recommend is trying to sell a premium offer directly from these emails. For example, sending people a link to a sales page for a $500 course or $2,000 coaching program probably won't work very well. You haven't built up enough connection, trust, and credibility at that point for people to jump in and buy a relatively expensive offer, sight unseen. The exception to this might be if someone is coming to you with a particularly urgent and important problem and they're willing to pay for a solution right away, even if there's some risk that it doesn't work out for them. Maybe you have a program that helps people deal with a particular type of HR issue that can cause a huge legal liability. They might be looking to sign up immediately because they need to deal with the issue right away. But these types of offers tend to be rare.

To determine what offer and call to action will work best for you, begin by thinking through who your customer is, what their needs and questions are, and what steps they need to go through to invest in the next stage of working with you.

JANE'S NURTURE SEQUENCE

Let's return to Jane's example, where her goal is to get people to opt in, keep them engaged, and ultimately book a call with her. Prospective clients would first sign up for her free mini-course. They'd then receive a series of emails, several of which would invite them to book a complimentary coaching call with Jane to discuss the assessment they completed in the mini-course, their signs of burnout, and where they might need help. As more people join the mini-course and begin to book calls, Jane starts to build a steady pipeline of clients.

APPLY IT

Now it's time to define your opportunities to engage prospective clients, and build trust, before you begin making paid offers.

Start by answering these key engagement questions:

- How will you nurture people after they sign up for your free course (or other resource)?

- What's the call to action? What are you asking people to do as you engage with them? Consider options such as a free coaching or Discovery call, a webinar, or a low-cost product such as a workbook or self-study course.

CHAPTER 5

REVENUE: RAMPING UP YOUR OFFERINGS & LEVERAGING YOUR TIME

WE STARTED THIS BOOK with the bad news: Courses aren't a silver bullet. Creating an online course doesn't mean you'll magically get customers, earn passive income, or grow your business. This chapter is about the *good* news: You can absolutely grow your revenue, and get more value from your limited time, by leveraging online courses in smart, strategic ways. The key is to be thoughtful in *how* you offer courses, and *where* they fit into your overall business model.

There are two primary ways to leverage online courses to earn revenue and grow your business:

1. Sell courses directly to customers.
2. Use courses to grow revenue from the services (coaching, consulting, outsourcing, etc.) you offer.

Pop quiz:

Which approach do you think is typically most impactful? Selling courses directly, or using courses to grow services revenue? Pause and take a moment to think about this, before I give you my perspective.

OK, got your answer? Here's mine: It all depends on your stage of business. Yes, sorry, it's the old "it depends!" answer. But it truly *does* depend on what stage you're in, your access to customers, and the demands on your time. For early-stage businesses — say, a coach who is just starting out — service revenue is typically the key to getting going. When you're first starting out, there's a clear cash imperative. You've got to bring in money *now* to pay the bills, not just have the potential for amazing revenue down the road.

As revenue grows, the equation begins to shift. Your time becomes stretched ever thinner, so bringing in revenue from more leveraged offerings — such as online courses and group coaching programs — becomes increasingly important. You're maxed out on time and you don't want any more appointments on your calendar, but you want to serve more people and continue growing your earnings. If you could sell courses on top of your existing services revenue, you could get the best of both worlds.

Take a moment now to think about where you are in your business:

- How many clients do you typically have each month?
- How much revenue did you earn in the past 12 months?
- How much do you expect to earn in the next 12 months?
- How maxed out are you on time? In a typical week, how

many hours are you spending on direct client service (for example, one-on-one coaching calls) or other meetings?

Based on your answers, consider which area you'd probably benefit the most from focusing on first: growing services revenue, or ramping up course revenue directly. Got your answer? Great! In the next sections, we'll explore specific approaches you can use.

STRATEGIES TO INCREASE REVENUE: SELLING COURSES DIRECTLY

A lot goes into selling an online course successfully — I could write a whole book just about that! And entire training programs are available online to help. For example, our partners at Mirasee offer a fantastic training called "Sell More Courses" with in-depth advice on over 20 different marketing strategies. So I'm not going to try to cover every approach under the sun, when such great resources are already available. Instead, I'll focus specifically on how you can *identify opportunities to increase revenue from a particular course offering.*

You can use the Course Revenue Optimization Model, seen here, to identify these opportunities. Let's take a look at the model and then we'll explore strategies for improving your course revenue based on the model.

THE COURSE REVENUE OPTIMIZATION MODEL

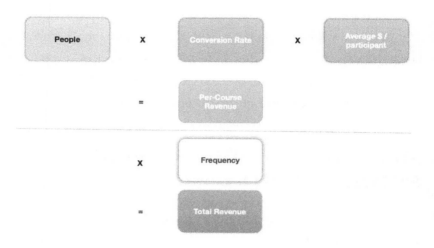

There are four key components to this model:

1. The number of people who see your course offer
2. The conversion rate
3. The average revenue per customer
4. How many offers you make over a period of time

Here's an example. Let's say you've built a mailing list of 1,000 people who are interested in your work and offerings. You then publish an online course and promote the offer to your list. If 2% of people sign up for the course (which would be a really solid conversion rate in most cases), you'd see around 20 sign-ups. Suppose your average customer pays $500 (different people might pay different amounts, which we'll explore in more detail shortly). That all multiplies out to $10,000 in revenue for this particular course promotion. You can also see that if you run this course twice a year, you could expect $20,000 in total revenue for the year ($10,000 x two promotions).

THE COURSE REVENUE OPTIMIZATION MODEL WITH EXAMPLE DATA

So that's all nice in the abstract, but what can you do with this model? The model's real value is that you can use it to identify opportunities for increasing revenue, by thinking through each of the four components. Start by asking these questions:

1. How can you increase the number of people who see your course offer?

2. How can you improve your conversion rate — the percentage of people who sign up for a given course?
3. How can you increase your average revenue per customer sign-up?
4. How can you offer your programs more frequently or more consistently so you have more chances to earn revenue over the course of the year?

APPLY THE COURSE REVENUE OPTIMIZATION MODEL TO IDENTIFY OPPORTUNITIES FOR INCREASING REVENUE

How do you increase revenue?

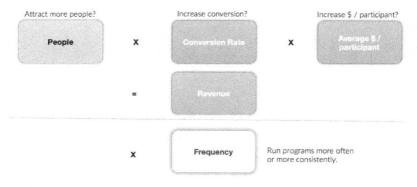

Opportunity Area 1: Increase the Number of People Who See Your Course Offer

This is a big area — huge, really! There are countless strategies you could try to attract more people to your website, your email list, and your course offerings. There are too many options to explore in great detail here. But for starters, I'd recommend considering the following strategies:

- **Partnerships.** Research people who provide related and complementary courses, but aren't competing directly with you on the same topic or course focus. Reach out to them about partnering to cross-promote your work.

- **Webinar swaps.** A specific form of partnership is a webinar swap, in which you offer to co-host a live teaching webinar for another expert. Then they reciprocate and host a webinar for you to present to their audience. You scratch their back, and vice versa. You and your partner both get to reach new people and build your mailing lists for future course offers.

- **Podcast outreach.** Identify podcasts that appeal to people who fit the profile of participants in your course. Reach out to the hosts about appearing as a guest. Most smaller podcasts are constantly on the hunt for interesting guests, so it's not too difficult to get booked, and it's a fabulous way to have your voice and expertise in front of new people.

- **Professional associations.** As discussed in Chapter 3, professional associations are an often-overlooked channel for reaching people specifically interested in your area of expertise. It's definitely worth researching relevant associations and reaching out to them about ways to partner and work together.

As mentioned earlier, we highly recommend the "Sell More Courses" program from our partners at Mirasee if you'd like to dive into other strategies for getting more people to see and purchase your courses. Check out https://sellmore.courses for details.

Opportunity Area 2: Improve Your Conversion Rate

One of the biggest untapped possibilities for generating more revenue is to improve your conversion rate — the percentage of people who sign up for your course offer. For most independent course creators, there are two big opportunities here: design an engaging promotional campaign and craft a more effective sales page.

DESIGN AN ENGAGING PROMOTIONAL CAMPAIGN

On February 28, 2008, acclaimed scholar and bestselling author Karen Armstrong received the TED Prize. This prize isn't just an honor; it's an opportunity to bring something new to life. And she did: She launched the Charter for Compassion, which is now a global nonprofit organization that shares its teachings with hundreds of thousands of members and students. Their mission is inspiring: to create a world where everyone is committed to living by the principle of compassion. But like many mission-driven organizations, the Charter for Compassion has had its challenges in reaching students and realizing revenue to support its mission.

When their team reached out to me a few years ago, they were already excited about the possibilities of using online courses to reach more people and increase their impact. They had set up a course on the Ruzuku learning platform and tried promoting it to their global email list, with tens of thousands of subscribers. And, unfortunately, they were deeply disappointed in the results. They expected their first course to generate huge excitement, interest, sign-ups, and sales. Instead, it was more like a trickle. So, what went wrong?

In their first launch, they promoted their course with the following activities:

- They sent two "announcement" emails to their general mailing list.
- They mentioned the course a couple of times on their main social media accounts.
- They set up a basic sales page with a summary of the course content.

When I met with the Charter for Compassion team and reviewed this initial promotion, I had to be pretty blunt. I told them this just wasn't going to cut it — they weren't doing nearly enough to get the attention and engagement of their audience. That was probably hard to hear after all the work they'd put in creating and offering the course, but they were eager to move forward and get better results, so they took my critique in stride.

Working together, we laid out an updated campaign:

- Draft a campaign of 10 emails to be sent over a four-week "launch window."
- Design new content to engage and interest people before

they sign up for the course, including a quiz, a video, and a simple game (worksheet-style, nothing too fancy or tech-heavy).

- Regularly mention the course on social media throughout the promotion.
- Write a much more detailed sales page with more interesting and persuasive content.

Here's the question for you: How did this second campaign perform? Did it get better results, and if so, by how much? You can probably guess that the second campaign was more successful, but you might be surprised at how *much* more successful. The difference, in fact, was staggering: The new campaign had nearly *10 times* as many sign-ups as the first attempt! Sadly, most people I speak with about their courses are running promotions much more like the first launch previously described (a couple of announcement emails) rather than the second one (a deep, well-planned campaign with engaging content).

Like the Charter for Compassion, you can improve your conversion rate and your revenue by crafting what I call a "wholehearted" campaign for your course. This term was inspired by Brené Brown's work on what she defines as "wholehearted" living and leadership. Specifically, a wholehearted approach entails cultivating authenticity, intuition, creativity, and meaningful work. You can apply this philosophy to your course promotion, by pouring your creative energy into your marketing campaign. In the case of the Charter for Compassion, I coached them to use their deep perspective on compassion and emotional intelligence to share valuable and engaging materials with their audience, including an inspiring video and a fun quiz. They weren't "pushing" for a sale; they were wholeheartedly sharing their teaching. And by doing so, they attracted far more people to their course.

So your mission is to plan a detailed promotion with an engaging email sequence for a specific course. Bear in mind that most people, just like the Charter for Compassion, underpromote their courses. So if you had decided to send two or three emails to "announce" or "promote" your course, challenge yourself to brainstorm what a sequence of 10 engaging, educational, and persuasive emails might look like. Specifically, you should follow the do's and don'ts listed here.

DON'T rely on "announcements."	DO educate and create intrigue.
DON'T give people opportunities only for passive, "consumptive" activities (viewing, reading, etc.).	DO inspire people to action (responding, commenting, completing a quiz, etc.).
DON'T focus solely on automation and "broadcasting" messages.	DO focus on engagement and personal connection, such as inviting people to reply to your emails or chat with you on your sales page.

To return to the example of Jane, the career coach, here's an example of how she might promote a program to her audience. As we mentioned before, part of her strategy is to run a leveraged group coaching program on goal-setting. Jane could schedule a session of her group program, and promote it with an email sequence along these lines:

Email number and angle	Subject line
Email #1: Announce Offer	The REAL reason you struggle with your goals
Email #2: Why Join?	What happens when your motivation wanes?
Email #3: The Potential	How to tackle your most ambitious goals
Email #4: New Identity	What kind of person are you?
Email #5: Be Your Own Hero	Imagine if...
Email #6: Crossroads	What happens if you do nothing
Email #7: Last Call	Go for Your Goals — before it's too late!

Planning this campaign also raises the question of how Jane would write high-quality, persuasive copy for these emails, if she's not a trained copywriter herself. This question brings up the "build versus buy" decision; in particular, if Jane should write all these emails herself, or look to source them from a professional provider. In Chapter 9 we'll explore how she can make that decision, for both her content and the supporting promotional emails. Regardless of whether Jane writes the emails herself or outsources them, her email campaigns need to be persuasive, with a clear focus on increasing her conversion rate.

CRAFT A MORE EFFECTIVE SALES PAGE

While putting together an engaging, interesting promotional sequence for your course is important, it's all for naught if the sales page that your customers ultimately see fails to get sign-ups. So your next step in improving conversion is to create a detailed, persuasive sales page that excites people and motivates them to sign up for your course. The only problem? That's *really* hard. I've been creating sales pages for years, and I still find it extremely challenging.

So where to start? There's one thing many people get wrong about sales pages: They focus on the "what" of the course, instead of connecting with potential customers at an emotional level. Just outlining the "nuts and bolts" of what content the course includes, and how it works, isn't likely to get people over the finish line. Information alone doesn't make the sale. That's why skilled copywriters are in such demand. That said, don't spend thousands of dollars on copywriters or your own copywriting training. Instead, let's start with a framework I've found incredibly helpful to write more resonant sales pages. It's called the "Love Letter Framework" and it's based on an inspiring article by Alexandra Franzen called "Stop making a 'sales pitch.' Instead, write your customer a 'love letter.'"

Here's how she describes the approach: "What if instead of writing a traditional 'sales pitch' about your latest product, service, event, project, workshop or offering, you simply wrote your customers...a Love Letter?" To get started, fill in your answers to these prompts:

- I want to live in a world where _____.
- I'm saddened when I hear from people who feel _____.
- I want you to _____.
- I've created a _____.
- I've designed this program to help you learn:
- Here's how we'll help you learn:
- Here's what we'll cover:
- Whom is this program for?
- Right now, I want you to:
  - o Register for a free call/webinar
  - o Buy now
  - o Join my early-access email list
  - o Apply / contact me

As you draft a sales page based on your love letter, be sure to make it as specific to your audience as possible. Here are some tips:

- Make your course title and sales page copy specific and compelling for your particular audience.

- Change words like *them*, *someone*, or *others* to be more specific to your market (e.g., *spouse, team, colleagues, children, clients*, etc.).

- Start sentences with customized phrases such as: "As a business owner," "As you become healthier," "As a divorced woman."

- End sentences with phrases that address the problem your audience is trying to solve, like "especially when communicating with your spouse" or "which matters even more when you are making progress toward better health."

- Add or change examples and stories to be specific to your audience (rather than targeted at a broad, general population).

Finally, make sure to include some key elements on your sales page:

- **Testimonials.** These are essential for providing credibility. If you haven't run a course (or this particular course) before, look at including testimonials from other offerings, such as coaching, in-person workshops, and so on. Choose quotes that focus more on your general qualities and expertise as opposed to the endorsement of a specific offer.

- **Your bio.** Don't forget to answer those basic questions of who you are and why someone should listen to you. Near the end of your online course sales page, include a short bio about yourself. The point is to assure your reader that you have the experience and knowledge to teach this course.

- **FAQ.** Before there's even a chance for them to get skeptical, answer some of your clients' most common questions. An FAQ section is usually a list of the 5 to 10 most common questions students have. The point of doing this is to help them overcome objections and concerns about taking your online course before they even have them.

- **A P.S.** Remember how I said some people will skim your page and just read the top and the bottom? For those skimmers, it's smart to include a short P.S.-style section at the end of your sales page. You can use this section to summarize or wrap up your online course sales page with a personal note and give them one last reason to enroll.

Your mission: Use this sales page format and these tips to craft a page that speaks directly to your intended audience, and bolsters the conversion rate of your course offering.

Opportunity Area 3: Increase Your Average Customer Value

Perhaps counterintuitively, increasing your average customer value is one of the most feasible strategies for increasing your course revenue. Increasing your conversion rate is certainly possible, but this approach can take a lot of experimentation to get right! In contrast, many people are "leaving money on the table" simply because they're underpricing their courses. Or they may be failing to take advantage of one of the most effective strategies for increasing average customer value: providing multiple price tiers.

THE POWER OF PRICE TIERS

While simple in concept — you've probably experienced price tiers yourself as a customer — few people use price tiers to their full potential. The idea here is straightforward: Create a "menu" of different price levels and allow your course participants to choose from this menu based on their own needs. Here's an example.

Choose your plan...	Standard Package	Premium Package	Launch Consulting Package
	Our step-by-step 4-week training, live calls, online discussion & resources.	Our step-by-step 4-week training PLUS follow-up calls, personal course review & email coaching.	Our step-by-step 4-week training PLUS personalized one-on-one consulting to help you get results, fast.
Core Learning Modules			
4 core learning modules, delivered through an online course (hosted on ruzuku, of course!).	✓	✓	✓
Weekly Live Calls + Chats			
Take advantage of the weekly presentations and group coaching sessions to motivate you, connect with others, and get your questions answered.	✓	✓	✓

This strategy of using price tiers allows you to build upon the course design and content you already have and offer significantly increased price points, without dramatically more work. At the same time, this approach is of great service to your customers. You're empowering them to opt in to the level of content and support they need. Each individual customer can choose, for example, if she wants to "go it alone" or get extensive hand-holding from you. For example, someone who is super-busy and having trouble fitting the course into her life may need a high degree of structure and accountability to keep progressing through your program. If her only option is the "self-study" or "group discussion" version of your program, she might fall by the wayside, or even choose not to sign up for your course in the first place! In contrast, a "VIP" or "private support" version of your program — with much stronger accountability and support — could give her the structure and support she needs.

So that's the concept. The devil, as always, is in the details. You'll need to think through different approaches for distinguishing your pricing options. There are six primary ways you can differentiate the price tiers in your courses:

1. **Live teaching versus self-study materials.** There's a big difference between going through an online course entirely on your own ("self-study"), compared to having a trusted instructor guide you through it with weekly teaching webinars, regular emails, check-ins, and so on. So one way to differentiate your price tiers is to offer a low-cost self-study option for people who need the most affordable way to access your material, with a higher-priced guided experience for people who value the richness of the live teaching experience.

2. **Access to specific materials or modalities.** Different people value access to your content in different forms, which opens up numerous possibilities for differentiation. You might create a nicely designed printed workbook that accompanies your course. In the premium price tier, you ship that physical workbook to participants so that they have it right at hand to guide their journey through the course. Or a meditation course's premium tier might include additional guided meditations as downloadable audio.

3. **Participation in peer learning and community.** Learning from a trusted instructor is important and powerful. But for many people, learning from others with similar needs — their peers in the course — is extremely valuable both for motivation, and for active, engaged learning. So another option is to facilitate online discussion and community (hosted on Ruzuku or another community platform) as part of your higher-end tiers.

4. **Personalized support, coaching, or consulting.** It's one thing to absorb techniques at a conceptual level, and quite another to actually implement the techniques. That's where support and coaching shine. By working with your clients directly, you can help hold them accountable, keep them on track, and redirect them when they're getting lost. This is also one of the easiest tiers to market and sell, because most customers will understand the value of personalized support or coaching.

5. **"Done for you" services.** Coaching and consulting are great, but the onus is still on the client to get things done. In many business contexts, clients need the work actually completed — not just a road map for *how* to complete it. It's worth assessing if this describes your work and course, and then thinking about what services you could provide to help your clients get to their end results. For example, if you teach social media marketing methods, you could offer a service in your high-end tier where you set up your client's social media profiles, create a schedule of posts for them, and so on.

6. **Follow-up after the initial course experience.** What happens after your course ends? Can you offer calls, ongoing community, and other opportunities?

To design your tiers, take some time to reflect on two key factors. First, what will be most supportive for your participants — what help and support do they need from you? Next, what can you provide without expending too much of your time and resources?

Opportunity Area 4: Increase the Consistency and Frequency of Your Offerings

The final opportunity is simple to describe, just not so simple to execute. To best serve your clients, and to grow revenue, you need to make offers for your programs and courses *consistently*. The key is to plan an offering calendar for each year. You can start by answering these questions:

- What are the key offers you want to promote over the next 12 months (consider courses, coaching packages, workshops, events, etc.)?
- Do you have partners, colleagues, or friends whose work you want to promote at specific times?
- Is there a sequence that's important to consider in your offering calendar? For example, do you have a progression from introductory course to more specialized courses, or advanced coaching/mentoring?
- What are your schedule constraints for the next 6–12

months? Consider how these might impact your ability to offer or run courses at specific times:

o   Vacations

o   Conferences

o   Speaking engagements

o   Moving

o   Family/health

o   Other constraints

Then, looking at the year week by week, lay out a tentative schedule of offerings that fits your priorities and sequencing. The further out you plan, the more tentative the schedule will be, and that's OK. There will also be uncertainty with new offerings, and that's OK too.

Here's how an example offer calendar might look for Jane:

January	Quarterly workshop: annual review and setting goals to kick off the year
February	Promote a colleague's new book
March	Group coaching program: spring session
April	Quarterly workshop: setting and achieving goals
May	Promote free mini-course (to build engagement and get new one-on-one coaching clients)
June	
July	Quarterly workshop: setting and achieving goals

August	Group coaching program: fall session
September	
October	Quarterly workshop: setting and achieving goals
November	Promote free mini-course (to build engagement and get new one-on-one coaching clients)
December	

By mapping out her offerings, Jane is able to achieve her goals of making offerings consistently and frequently, which will multiply her revenue. Many coaches and course creators I speak with take more of a "fly by the seat of my pants" approach, deciding week by week what offers to make and what promotions to launch. While it can be nice to have flexibility at times, this approach is overly optimistic. The reality is, you'll typically get busy with client work and other commitments, and be unable to make as many offers as you'd originally hoped. That's why it's so critical to plan your offer calendar in advance to target your desired frequency of offerings. As they say, if you fail to plan, you're planning to fail. Instead, make a plan so you can grow your revenue — month by month, and year by year.

STRATEGIES TO INCREASE REVENUE: GROWING SERVICES REVENUE WITH COURSES

Now let's turn to how you can expand your services revenue, using courses as a vehicle to invite people into relevant services packages. Services are the workhorse of your business, providing consistent cash flow and the foundation for more leveraged offerings, such as premium courses and other products. For early-stage businesses (say, roughly, less than $100,000 in annual revenue), your top priority should generally be to bring in consistent, profitable services revenue. Here are three strategies for using courses to grow this essential revenue stream.

Opportunity Area 1. Provide a Personalized Worksheet Review That Leads to a Coaching Offer

Worksheets are a powerful way to help participants take action in a free course, and also to lay the groundwork for their interest in a coaching package or other service. You can provide a worksheet that elicits the participant's challenges through questions and prompts. Then offer to review their worksheet responses on a 20-minute call, which is free for them to book. The idea is they're coming to this call prepared with their worksheet and ready to discuss their challenges and needs. It's a variation on the approach of offering a free strategy or Discovery call, but using the worksheet as the focus of the session.

Orienting the session around the worksheet review makes it more concrete and appealing for someone to book a call and provides a clear focus. You can flow naturally from discussing their challenges and next steps based on the worksheet responses to a service offer that would meet their needs. For example, Jane could review someone's worksheet responses about their career goals, and then introduce a coaching package that would help them move forward toward achieving those goals.

Opportunity Area 2. Integrate Upsells to Service Packages via Links and Buttons

A simple option for selling services in a free or low-cost course is to include direct upsell links in content and activities throughout the course. The strategy is to help people get value from your techniques, then show them an offer to go deeper with a premium service package. Think about the flow of how people would progress through the program, and identify at what point they would likely be open to an offer to go deeper in working with you. You're not hammering them with an offer as soon as they join the course; you're presenting the offer at a logical and relevant time.

One small but impactful tip: To provide a strong call to action, consider including a graphical button (rather than just a text link) in your activity. Have that button link to a page with more information about your offer. On that offer page, you should address one of the key challenges with services, which is that they're something you can buy "at any time." And when you can buy something at any time, there's absolutely no urgency to buy right now. Your prospective client may be thinking, "That coaching sounds really cool, maybe I'll do it next week…next month…next year…"

So how do you create a strong reason to sign up for your service offering now, rather than risk having potential clients procrastinating endlessly? A great technique is to offer a special package, rather than open-ended coaching or services. If it fits with your calendar, you can make this a time-limited offer that you update throughout the year. For example, a health coach might offer a special "New Year's Health Resolution Package." She'd invite new clients to sign up by a specific date (say, January 31 of each new year) to get this package. Ideally, the package should contain more than just coaching. So she might also offer to ship a special edition of her daily health journal to new clients. Now she's converting an open-ended services offer into a compelling, time-limited package that motivates a potential client to sign up right away.

Opportunity Area 3. Host group Q&A or Coaching Calls with a Special Offer

"Underpromise and overdeliver." That simple framework is the key to exceeding your client's expectations. While you may have applied this concept in the context of your paid coaching or other services, it's often overlooked when it comes to delivering free offerings. Yet there's a great opportunity here. If you can "overdeliver" or "wow" participants in a free course that you offer for lead generation, you'll have a far greater chance of converting those people into paying clients.

What I've found particularly effective is to offer live webinars or calls in your free programs. These live interactions are a great way to engage with people, and participants often aren't expecting this in a free or low-cost course — so you win on the "exceeding expectations" front. You're providing a genuinely valuable opportunity for people to ask you questions and get help. But it's also a great marketing opportunity for you, because people are so attentive and engaged during these calls. You can offer these calls via a tool of your choice (Zoom, Google Meet, Ruzuku's built-in teleconferencing, etc.). Importantly, you should plan to integrate a call to action into these events. Invite attendees to sign up for a special offer, such as a service package (structured using the tips previously described), or a premium course.

APPLY IT

Reflect on these questions:

What is your best opportunity to increase each of the following?
- Visitors
- Conversion
- Average revenue
- Frequency and consistency of your offerings

How could you use courses to sell more of your coaching, consulting, or other services?

CHAPTER 6

RETENTION: LONG-TERM CUSTOMER VALUE

BACK IN 2013, I had a breakthrough, a classic "aha moment."

We'd been offering our online course platform, Ruzuku, for a couple of years at that point. We were bringing more customers on board and growing our company step by step, but everything from the product to our marketing was still embryonic. So it was a big moment when we launched our first premium training program for course creators (with the highly creative name of "30 Days to Your Online Course"). I was excited to ramp up this new revenue stream and thrilled to help our customers learn how to create a course so they could jump ahead in their businesses.

A curious thing kept happening during the training sessions, though. People kept asking questions like "Now what? I know how to create my course but how do I get the word out? How do I market it? Where do I begin? What works? What's a waste of time?" So, we quickly pulled together another paid training — called "No Empty

Seats" — to answer these questions. Several of our participants enrolled so they could learn how to market their online courses and keep moving ahead with their goals. Then a few super-ambitious entrepreneurs from "No Empty Seats" stepped into private consulting with me. They wanted to go all out on their online course businesses and were happy to pay for the intensive, personalized training they needed.

Here's what surprised me: The combined revenue we earned from "No Empty Seats" and consulting was far more than what we earned for "30 Days to Your Online Course." We *more than doubled* our original training revenue because we offered additional opportunities to our eager customers. We were fulfilling our customers' precise needs and aspirations to serve their clients, grow their businesses, and enjoy greater success with their online courses.

And the major aha moment? Keeping your *existing* customers coming back for more is the secret to achieving consistent, sustainable revenue growth. You've probably heard that it's much easier (and more cost-effective!) to *keep* a customer than to *acquire* a customer. But the tricky part for many coaches and course creators I speak with is that they don't have a system to retain and serve their customers over the long run. This means that, after all the hard work they do (and money they invest) to attract and enroll customers, they're sacrificing a huge amount of potential *long-term* revenue.

I don't want this to happen to you! So, in this chapter, we'll explore why customer retention is so important. Then we'll dive into how you can better retain and serve your customers by helping them progress on their journey after they begin working with you.

CUSTOMER LIFETIME VALUE

In Chapter 2, we introduced the concept of customer lifetime value (CLTV). This metric measures how valuable a customer is to your business over time.

Many companies use CLTV to identify their most lucrative customers so they can focus on attracting more like them to grow their business. CLTV also helps you apply the fundamental principle that retaining existing, profitable customers is more cost-efficient and financially rewarding than onboarding new clients. Here are the key points to keep in mind as you apply this concept in your business:

1. Don't worry about making a profit on a low-priced, entry-level product (such as a $97 mini-course) if you can eventually enroll those buyers into higher-ticket services and programs (like a $2,000 group program).

2. Don't make unfounded assumptions about who will be an ideal long-term-value customer. People you'd never suspect would be ready to write a big check for a high-ticket program can surprise you! That said, your goal is to spend your time serving clients who are ready to move beyond your freebies, books, and low-ticket offers.

3. Study the patterns of your highest-value customers: What do they have in common? Why do they keep coming back for more? What are their common beliefs, challenges, desires? What is the transformation they seek to achieve? The more you get curious and dig into questions like these, the

more you'll be able to fine-tune your offerings to meet the needs and demands of high-value customers, which in turn will increase your CLTV over time.

DESIGN THE PATH

Now that we're clear on the importance of retaining your customers, you need a plan to do it. The best way to start is to lay out a Retention Path for your clients to follow. Your job is to add value and help clients achieve deeper results at each step on the path.

Avoid creating another offer just so you have something new to sell. Instead, seek to plot a sequence of offers that's logical and compelling from your customer's point of view. Each successive offer should build on what the customer learned and achieved in your prior course or program. It should address the *next set* of problems, questions, and desires that result from their new level of awareness and skill.

You'll design your Retention Path by asking this fundamental question, again and again: *What's the next step?*

Putting yourself in your customer's shoes, ask: "*What's the next step for me on my path toward my goals?*"

To answer this question, first dig deep to understand your ideal customers' current situation. Begin by asking questions such as:

- What's causing them pain or frustration?
- What problems do they want to solve?
- What challenges, whether physical or emotional, are holding them back?

For example, if you're a dating coach, your ideal customers might be divorced women over 50 who are tired of spending lonely weekends by themselves, but are too scared to try online dating. Or say you're a health coach, and your ideal customers are successful startup entrepreneurs who are overweight and feel sluggish because they can't break away from the long days and breakneck pace of their responsibilities.

Once you understand your customers' current problems and frustrations, you can then consider the full scope and context of what your customer is trying to achieve, by asking:

- *What are their goals, dreams, and aspirations?*
- *What is the transformation they seek, and what does it look and feel like from their perspective?*

For the older divorced woman, her dream could be to get back in the dating scene, to meet vibrant, kind, honest men and feel confident and relaxed on each date. At this point, the transformation she seeks might be as simple as just dating again and having more fun. For the overworked entrepreneur, the initial result they might long for is to drop 15 pounds so they feel lighter, look better, and have more energy to exercise and keep up with their grueling work schedule.

Now that you're clear on your customers' current situation, challenges, and goals, you'll want to determine the key results of your offer. These results, *combined*, will help people achieve the transformation they desire.

For our dating example, key results could include:

1. Get clear in your expectations for a dating partner so you don't waste time or energy chasing down rabbit holes with the wrong men.
2. Assess your personal values, your strengths, and what makes life sweet so you feel clear and confident about what you offer.
3. Learn how to write an engaging dating app profile that filters out the wrong types and attracts exactly the kind of men you'd love to meet.

For the health coaching example, key results could include:

1. Assess eating habits and food choices to better understand the culprits that could be contributing to your excess weight.
2. Discover ways to sneak in 30 minutes of exercise a day to recharge your energy even when work is wild.
3. Build new boundaries for self-care to create a sense of control over your day and ensure you get the life-enhancing exercise you need.

Then think about the next step after these initial results are achieved. Once your customer completes your course, coaching program, or other experience, what's the next step for them? What will make their life even better? Answering these questions will help you design your next offer and build out a Retention Path to keep your customers coming back for more.

To revisit our dating example, once the customer starts dating again and meeting some great guys (the initial goal), the next goal might be to unearth and transform any mindset and behavioral patterns that could lead to repeating past mistakes and sabotaging a new relationship. For the health coaching example, once the client drops 15 pounds and starts to feel more energized, the next goal could be to layer in lifestyle passions that promote exercise, joy, and even longevity, such as bicycling, gardening, and forest bathing.

Now, plotting out an effective Retention Path requires reflection and planning. It requires additional deep assessment of your customers' situation, challenges, and desires at each stage as they progress through each of your courses or programs. This strategy likely requires you to create new offers — just as Ruzuku had to create our "No Empty Seats" training.

I realize you might not have a Retention Path in place today — don't worry, you're not alone. Typically, when I look at people's offers, I point out that they've created more of a "library" model. They have a library of courses to sell, but these offers don't necessarily fit together into a logical sequence that helps clients progress from one step to the next. So if that's where you find yourself today, that's totally fine. (At the same time, please don't get overwhelmed by the idea you have to build everything for your customers' retention journey from scratch. You may be able to leverage some of the materials you've already created. And you may also be able to incorporate prebuilt, professionally designed course content materials, which is a subject we'll explore in Chapter 9.)

Just bear in mind that if you want to retain more of your customers and enjoy more abundant and consistent revenue coming into your business, the big opportunity ahead of you is to map out a compelling, effective Retention Path for your customers. Let's take a look at two more examples to see how.

Stress Reduction Example

Say you have a course on helping people manage and reduce stress. Your initial course teaches how to achieve the following results:

1. Implement mindfulness into your daily routine so you can calm worry and anxiety, and feel more in control no matter what's happening around you.
2. Keep a daily stress journal so you can understand your stress manifestation patterns and identify your personal stress triggers.
3. Use gratitude practices to build and maintain a more positive mindset, and deal with stress in a more resilient, relaxed manner.

Once participants achieve these initial course goals, we return to the key question: *What's next?*

-   What does the participant want next on their stress reduction journey?
-   What's still missing in their knowledge and skill set?
-   What other problems do they want to overcome?

- What other transformation or dream would they like to achieve?
- And what can you offer to address their needs and desires?

You might find people need help dealing with acute stress in a specific situation. For example, say your ideal customers work with a toxic boss or co-worker and they can't escape cutting, nerve-wracking comments and behaviors. How could they better handle those stressful moments? What would make life better for them? What support could you provide to get them to that next level of mastery in handling acute stress?

Perhaps you could offer an intimate group program focused on using meditation and breathing exercises to reduce stress in key moments. You could help participants apply these stress-reducing techniques by sending inspiring daily email reminders, holding bi-weekly group coaching calls, and providing 10 minutes of daily emergency text message coaching for each participant, Monday through Friday.

And for graduates of that group program who are still looking for more? You could enroll them into an alumni membership community to keep the supportive relationships and camaraderie going. Or for those seeking a more intensive, personalized path, you could offer private coaching that helps them dig into why they might end up in these toxic situations, establish new work relationship boundaries, and even set out to look for a new job.

Business Marketing Example

Let's look at another Retention Path example to drive this concept home. Say your primary course teaches students about Facebook marketing, with a focus on using a personal Facebook page to generate leads and create greater visibility for your business.

The initial course might help participants achieve the following key results:

1. Discover the 12 key types of content to grow and engage their audience.
2. Create a 6-month content calendar that aligns with their promotions so they stay focused and maximize their marketing results.
3. Leverage Facebook Messenger to build relationships, connect with potential leads, and boost the visibility of their content to a wider audience.

Once participants achieve these initial course goals, you'd again ask the key question: What's next?

- What else does the participant want to learn about Facebook marketing?
- What's still missing in their knowledge and skill set?
- What other problems do they want to overcome?
- What other transformation or dream would they like to achieve?
- What can you offer to address their needs and next level of growth?

Let's say your ideal customers are business-to-business consultants. They're likely eager to find more ways to demonstrate their expertise, provide more value to their community, and generate more leads to fill their group programs or one-on-one services. Why not offer a more advanced course on building hyper-engaged Facebook groups? You could show people how to leverage their personal Facebook page marketing techniques with a Facebook group. You could help them create a content calendar for their Facebook group. And you could teach them how to use a Facebook live training series to promote their offers to their loyal, eager community.

After that?

Perhaps start by offering one or more highly focused, complementary programs that strengthen the specific skills people need to master Facebook marketing. Consider the foundational skills that would help them take a significant leap forward in everything else you're teaching. For example, you could help people zero in on their ideal customer avatar, stand out in a sea of look-alike experts, or package irresistible offers so they can ramp up their revenue and enjoy more wealth and freedom.

Then you could help your customers take another big leap by showing them how to facilitate online challenges inside their Facebook group. You'd help them use challenges to boost their group size, offer greater value to their members, increase their credibility, and test new offers before they do a full-scale launch.

Now that we've examined these two examples, remember that your overall goal as you design your Retention Path is to provide offerings that speak to the core needs, questions, and desires of your customers so they can keep making progress with each course or program they take with you. In fact, jumping into the next course with you should feel like the most obvious thing in the world! Also keep in mind that *not* offering a next-step course or program would be doing your customers a disservice. They have a need and a dream, and either you can fill it for them (and enjoy creating greater impact and the additional revenue that goes along with it) or they'll go to somebody else who can. So why miss out?

CREATING AN ASCENSION MODEL

Your goal is to build an integrated suite of offerings that customers can grow into as they work with you. With each successive offer in your Retention Path, you enhance the value and results you provide, as well as increase the price you charge. This progression of offers is sometimes called an "ascension model," and you can use it in designing your Retention Path.

Here's an illustration of a Retention Path that incorporates an ascension model:

STEP 1 — Free Access: blogs, webinars, videos, podcasts, and other free lead magnets.

STEP 2 — Low-Cost Products ($10 – $100): books, journals, newsletter subscriptions, self-study online courses, membership communities.

STEP 3 — Higher-Value Offerings ($100 – $2,000): cohort-based online courses with instructor feedback, in-person or virtual bootcamps, seminars, group coaching programs.

STEP 4 — Intensive Programs ($2,000 – $20,000+): These can include either group programs (masterminds, elite coaching groups, done for you services) or personalized support (private, one-on-one coaching or consulting).

Step 1 of this Retention Path is content you publish, including your blogs, videos, and podcasts, as well any free lead magnets you offer in exchange for an email address, such as checklists, guides, and quizzes. These free items are designed to entice people into your world, excite them with your viewpoint so they keep coming back, build your authority, and help you stay top of mind with your audience. They're also essential because, typically, people don't want to jump in and start working with someone they don't know at a high price point. In other words, someone is unlikely to stumble across your website and immediately sign up for a $2,000 coaching package. More often they prefer to start with an accessible, affordable offer and experience some initial progress. Then, when they're thinking, "Wow, this is working great. I want more!" they're ready to "ascend" to the next step.

Step 2 of your Retention Path includes low-ticket items, such as books, products, newsletter subscriptions, DIY courses, and membership communities. These are usually a no-brainer for people to invest in if they like the topic. They also continue to build your authority and relevance in the eyes of your customers, and prime them to want more of what you offer — to come further into your world.

The next is ascending to Step 3: higher-value, pricier offerings such as cohort-based online courses with instructor feedback, in-person or virtual bootcamps, seminars, and group coaching programs. If you can help a customer have success at this stage of the Retention Path, you're likely to build a strong personal bond and solidify your position as a preferred guide and expert.

Step 4 of the Retention Path includes intensive programs with deep personal support. These could be either group programs (masterminds, elite coaching groups, done for you services) or personalized support offerings (private, one-on-one coaching or consulting). In either model, the expectation is that you're providing much greater transformative support, and a more intimate and intensive experience for your customers. Your price should reflect that.

Many coaches and consultants I meet practically give their time away in low-priced, pay-as-you-go sessions. If you're doing that now, don't despair. Adopting what I'm sharing with you in this chapter and throughout this book will help you break free of that pattern so you can start charging according to the value of what you truly offer. Providing more intensive offerings that solve bigger problems and promise greater transformation can increase the long-term value of your customers. What's more, your customer retention will improve when your path of offerings better matches their exact needs, questions, and goals.

Let's review two examples to see how you can build an effective Retention Path that guides clients to ascend from one offer to the next. The first example is from Ruzuku's paid training and services

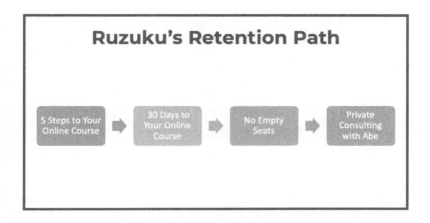

Ruzuku's first Retention Path was a success because:

1. Our free gift, "5 Steps to Your Online Course," provided quick wins and helped build trust with our audience. For a good number of people, that was enough to jump into our paid training.

2. The "30 Days to Your Online Course" program helped people just starting out. Most of the participants had an idea for a course, but didn't know how to get it started or set up.

3. For people who were successful in the "30 Days" course and ready to move forward, "No Empty Seats" helped them launch their course and market it successfully.

4. A few people in "No Empty Seats" wanted an intensive, personalized experience to learn and apply the marketing tactics beyond the initial framework. I provided private consulting to support them.

So not only was Ruzuku helping more and more people achieve the results that mattered most to them, but we were adding significant incremental revenue without having to go out and recruit a bunch of new customers. Remember, this particular Retention Pathway more than doubled our training revenue in the year we launched it. That's how powerful this strategy can be!

Here's another real-world example, from our partners at Mirasee.

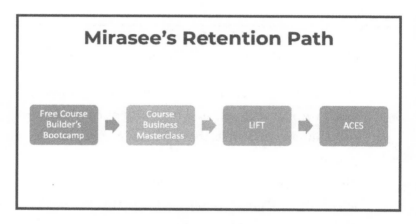

Danny Iny of Mirasee used Retention Paths to teach more than 5,000 students how to start and grow their own profitable, impactful online course businesses. Here's how Mirasee's current Retention Pathway works:

1. Mirasee's free, six-day "Course Builder's Bootcamp" is an easy entry point for any entrepreneur thinking about offering a course. It builds trust and leaves participants eager for more support.

2. The premium "Course Business Masterclass" helps participants get everything they need to go from zero to launching their first pilot course, making their first sale — and beyond. This course is a perfect foundation for what comes next: LIFT.

3. LIFT is a high-value, three-day event with a modest ticket price that gives course builders major breakthroughs along with a road map to consistent six- or seven-figure annual income. The event is an epic trust builder, and is Mirasee's launchpad for its exclusive ACES Club.

4. The ACES Club is Mirasee's top-tier, high-ticket, application-only offering that gives members a year of intensive training, coaching, community, and accountability.

At each level, Mirasee offers deeper and deeper value, builds greater levels of trust, and empowers participants to build thriving, successful online course businesses. As clients ascend from one step to the next, Mirasee charges more for its programs to reflect the higher value it provides and the increasingly transformative results people experience.

GUIDELINES FOR DESIGNING YOUR RETENTION PATH

Now, as you plot out your own customer's Retention Path, keep the following guidelines in mind.

Avoid Information Overload

Your Retention Path should be as simple as possible. Many new course creators inadvertently wind up creating "information overload" for their participants. They want to provide massive value in their first course or coaching program (which is great!) but they overdeliver and end up falling into three dangerous traps. First, creating an extremely large, in-depth course will take an extremely long time, and there's even a risk that you never actually get it done! Second, this "everything and the kitchen sink" course isn't going to be a good learning experience for your customers because there will be too much for them to absorb and too much work to implement the techniques. Third, this approach doesn't work as a business model.

As you've been learning in this chapter, you should seek to take people from one result to the next, from one transformation to the next. And customers should be paying you for that progress. So don't teach everything you know inside a single $400 course. You'd be overwhelming your customers, and you'd be giving away all your power and knowledge in one go. Then what would you have left to offer?

Get Into Your Customer's Point of View

I talked earlier about considering your offers from your customer's point of view, but let's take it further here. As you're reflecting on what offers to provide at each step of your Retention Path, ask yourself these questions:

- What challenges, questions, and desires do my customers have at each new step?
- What support can I provide to help them move forward step after step?

It'll be a big help if you get into your customer's point of view while doing this. Here are some of my favorite tricks for taking your customer's perspective:

- **Testimonials**. At the end of your course, ask participants what they found most valuable, and what problems the course helped them solve. Ask if they learned what they expected to learn, and whether they achieved the goals or transformation they were seeking. You can also ask for their suggestions to make your course an even better experience for others.

- **Assessments.** Ask your participants to complete an assessment of their challenges, problems, and desires before they begin your course, and at the end of the course. This will give you a clearer picture of how clients are growing and progressing.

- **Bonus Sessions.** When the end of your course is drawing near, schedule a special 20- or 30-minute bonus call with each of your participants. Then use that session to talk about their progress, their breakthroughs, the gaps they still have, and what they feel are their next steps. Not only will you gain critical insights, but you'll also have an opportunity to help them see how they can continue working with you.

- **Inbound Questions.** Collect questions from customers and people who didn't sign up for your offers. Also make sure to log questions you receive through email, social media, personal networking, and while on sales calls. These questions can provide huge insight about people's pain points, problems, and desires.

You can use these four methods to develop a deep understanding of your customer's point of view and experience. Then build off that understanding to identify ways to improve retention over time.

THE FIVE CORE RETENTION MODELS

So far in this chapter, we've seen lots of examples of how you can create your own Retention Path. In many cases, we've referred to "courses," but your next-step offering doesn't have to be a course! After all, course-building can be a labor-intensive exercise, and you can leverage your time and energy by offering your expertise in other ways as well. In this section, we'll explore the five core retention models you can choose from to build the right Retention Path for your ideal customers and business.

And while you're at it, keep these questions in mind:

- What would provide the most engaging and transformative experience for your ideal customers?

- What teaching model will best address their needs, implement what you teach, and keep them moving forward at each stage of your Retention Path?

- What models are the most energizing and rewarding for you to deliver?

Ready? Let's explore each of the five models. We'll use our stress reduction example to illustrate how each can work. This time, however, let's focus on a different customer niche: people who are stressed because they're trying to balance their life while taking care of a sick or elderly parent.

Membership or Community

Membership groups bring people together with a focused theme and common interests. In the stress reduction example, you might consider offering a free Facebook group designed for working women torn between the call of duty at home and the desire to do everything in their power to take care of their aging parent. You could provide valuable content, inspiring posts, and weekly live training tips to help them better cope with time management and the guilty feelings that can arise as they find out it's practically impossible to "do it all."

A next step along the Retention Path could be a paid membership community, where you offer more value, such as online workshops, organized networking, and guest experts once or twice a month. For our stress reduction example, your ideal members would likely enjoy the opportunity to mingle with kindred spirits who really get them. They'd also appreciate having access to practical tools for dealing with the stressful tension between all their work and home-life responsibilities and caring for a parent.

One challenge with memberships and paid communities is that, because they're typically free or low-cost, there's less "stickiness," less pressure on participants to engage, and less commitment over time. You can expect a degree of turnover, so it's important to keep inviting people in to replenish and grow membership.

Events: In-Person or Virtual Retreats or the Like

Most coaches, consultants, and other experts I've spoken to have been to a bunch of retreats or other events, either in-person, on-line, or both. My guess is that you have too, so you're probably well aware of the inspirational and transformative power these events can offer.

You can plan events — live or virtual — that range from 30-minute workshops delivered at the local chamber of commerce, to half- or whole-day intensive sessions tackling a specific problem, to a three-day transformative retreat (such as Mirasee offers with their LIFT conference, which helps course creators build a road map to a six- or seven-figure business).

Align the length and focus of your event with your audience's needs. Because time is pressed for women trying to take care of an aging parent while working and raising their own family, a three-hour virtual retreat might be stretching the limits of their constrained schedules. On the other hand, it might be just the thing to rejuvenate their spirits, help them feel seen and heard, and provide them with practical ideas.

Events and retreats are usually powerhouses of inspiration and breakthroughs. As soon as people leave the event, though, the euphoria wears off as "normal" life takes hold again. That's why smart marketers know to make an offer to attendees to *continue* what they learned *at the event* so they can start implementing the breakthroughs they experienced, and create lasting, measurable transformation.

More Advanced or Specialized Courses

Advanced and specialized courses are the perfect answer for participants who want to master a specific skill or strategy. It's assumed (and can even be required) that they've already learned and implemented the foundational skills so they can keep pace with the instructor and other attendees. Examples of specialized courses include creating a TEDx stage–worthy keynote talk, building an in-demand podcast, or learning how to make French pastry.

A specialized group program could also be just the thing for stressed-out working women whose parent has passed on or moved into a long-term care facility. These women would benefit greatly from the support such a group would provide to help them move through lingering grief, reenergize their health, and start framing out a new "normal" life that's meaningful and fulfilling.

"Stickiness" is high in advanced or specialized courses, especially if the group is limited to under 50 or so participants, and they get direct access to you in your group training and coaching sessions.

And because this is a highly engaging model, it's easier to draw participants into a complementary or next-level program. For instance, you might create a specialized course for caregivers on how to navigate the bewildering world of health insurance reimbursements.

Mastermind Groups

Mastermind groups hold participants' feet to the fire: There's no place to hide. These hyper-intensive, intimate groups teach, coach, and hold members accountable as they work toward implementing a common purpose, whether that's writing and launching a bestselling nonfiction business book, creating and marketing a high-ticket group program, or using Facebook as an authority-building and lead generation machine to increase prior-year income fourfold. (Yes, these are all real examples!)

For stressed-out women caring for an ill or aging parent, a mastermind group might be exactly what they need to finally enlist help from other family members to take more responsibility at home *and* care for the elderly parent, as well as to create and enforce self-care boundaries to preserve their own health and spirits for the long haul.

Masterminds are extraordinarily high on the "stickiness" scale. Because of the intimacy of the group and the focus on implementation of common goals, there's no room for "passive" consumption. Participation is essential, and accountability is a major priority. People who sign up typically crave that support — they want the group to push them to make significant progress, to move past problems and roadblocks, and to bring their goals and desires to fruition.

One-on-One Coaching or Consulting

You're probably aware that Tony Robbins, the renowned motivational speaker and author, offers his own ascension path of events, coaching programs, and masterminds to his audience — each pricier than the last, as you gain greater access to him. Did you also know that he charges about $1,000,000 to work with him one-on-one for a year? Nice work, if you can get it. While most of us will never be able to charge fees even close to that level, there's a valuable lesson you can take away from his example: Value your time as the precious gift it is.

That means positioning one-on-one time to reflect its impact and value. Clients will be tapping directly into your *years and years* of experience, and your education and training, for which you likely paid an enormous sum. You are a high-value, high-impact guide for them! So the investment to work directly with you ought to reflect that value.

Shifting your mindset about this might take some work — but you can do it. I know coaches, consultants, and experts who've made the shift and it was the best thing they ever did for their business. One of my favorite examples is a spiritual business coach who used to earn about $20,000 a year — total. Once she recognized how truly gifted she is, she raised her prices again and again, and is now charging $1,000 an *hour* for private coaching. And she's worth every penny of that to her happy customers.

Now, what could you offer our stress reduction customers in terms of one-on-one coaching? You might design a personalized, six-month journey to help them implement the life "redesign" they outlined in your advanced course. That way, you'd be there to coach and hold them accountable to their goals, inspire them when they fall, and ensure they come out the other side actually living the life they dreamed of.

One-on-one coaching is also incredibly "sticky." If your customers have a transformative experience, they may stick around for years to work with you — in your masterminds, membership communities, or specialized programs. They'll want to grab everything you offer because they know firsthand how much you changed their life for the better.

JANE'S EXAMPLE

Now let's see how Jane could build her Retention Path for her customers. She has many options, but here's a typical example:

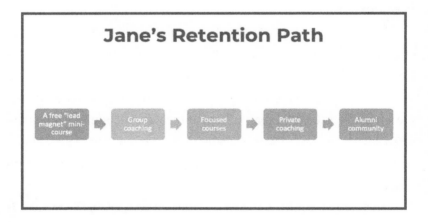

1. **Free "lead magnet" mini-course.** As a career and life coach, Jane could entice people into her world by offering a free lead magnet such as "10 Warning Signs You've Outgrown Your Career." Each mini-lesson could be one of the warning signs, which would be valuable both for people new to this concern, and for those who are already aware at some level that they're no longer happy in their work.

2. **Group coaching.** For people who grabbed her mini-course and realize that they have one foot out the door of their current career, they're now primed to want to know *how* to start evaluating new career choices. They're not ready to leave their job yet because they're not certain what would be the most satisfying new direction. But inside Jane's group coaching program, which includes training, resources, and group coaching calls, that's exactly what they'll discover.

3. **Focused courses.** No matter how good one's job is, work is a stressful place to be! For that reason, Jane could offer a suite of focused courses to help her customers deal with the daily grind. For example, she could help people learn to reduce stress at home using meditation, or to use mindfulness and meditation at work to diffuse tense situations. She could also offer a course to tame perfectionism and procrastination so her clients could make progress on their jumble of responsibilities and feel satisfied with their contributions.

4. **Private coaching.** For people eager to start making their new life and career happen as quickly as possible, private coaching is a perfect choice. Building on the results

customers attained in her group program, Jane could offer a nine-month private coaching program to help people hone their preferences, craft a powerhouse resume, learn how to use job boards effectively, discover secret ways to tap referral partners, have knockout interviews, and hit the ground running in their new career.

5. **Alumni community.** Once customers complete Jane's private coaching program, they'll benefit from connecting and networking with other alumni to share referrals, resources, career advice, and more. Jane can pop in and do live mini-trainings a couple times a month to offer timely tips for succeeding with a new career. She can invite guest speakers to share their wisdom. And Jane can offer periodic "office hours" so alumni can get coaching to keep them in top shape at work.

APPLY IT

Your turn! Now that you've learned why it's critical to retain your customers for the long term, and how to design a Retention Path, it's time to implement what you've discovered.

Reflect on these questions:

- Putting yourself in your customer's shoes, ask from their perspective, "What's the next step for me on my path toward my goals?"
  - o What's causing them pain or frustration?

- *o*   What problems do they want to solve?
- *o*   What challenges, whether physical or emotional, are holding them back?
- Once you understand your customer's current problems and frustrations, then consider the full scope and context of what your customer is trying to achieve.
  - *o*   What are their goals, dreams and aspirations?
  - *o*   What is the transformation they seek, and what does it look and feel like from their perspective?
- What are the key results of your course that, *combined*, will help people achieve the transformation they desire?
- Once your customer completes your course, coaching program, or other experience, what's the next step for them? What will make their life even better?

Finally, draw from the menu of retention models to choose the next logical, compelling step in your customer's journey.

CHAPTER 7

REFERRAL: THE GREATEST MARKETING CHANNEL IS WORD OF MOUTH

HOW CAN YOU make your business sustainable, enjoyable, and profitable for the long haul?

That's the question so many coaches, consultants, and solo entrepreneurs struggle with. I experienced this challenge myself in the early days of my career, when I launched a consulting business providing user experience (UX) design services. What I wanted — and what I'm guessing you want as well — was to grow consistently through happy customers and word of mouth. Those "warm" referrals are far easier and less stressful to maintain than pounding the (virtual) pavement to drum up new clients every week. Ideally, you'd work hard to build up a base of delighted customers. With that base established, the momentum starts a flywheel — you begin to get more referrals and eager prospects from your existing client roster, rather than trying to get meetings and close sales with people who've never heard of you before. As author David Greer has noted, "A customer talking about their experience with you is worth ten times that which you write or say about yourself."

I understood that concept, but I didn't know how to get this flywheel going. Instead, it felt like I was constantly pushing the proverbial boulder up a hill. (Perhaps Sisyphus was also a consultant?) It was an ordeal to find, get in touch with, and close a deal with each new client. Existing clients were pleased with the work I did, but the referrals just weren't pouring in. It turns out, it's not enough to *just* do good work in your area of expertise. You need to make it easy for people to refer others to you. This is the fifth and final phase of the Customer Learning Journey Model: Referral.

In this chapter, we'll explore how you can get more referrals using two different types of strategies. First, there are "bootstrapping" or small-scale strategies, which will help as you're starting out and beginning to grow an education- and service-based business. Next, we'll discuss "scaling" strategies that will help accelerate referrals in the context of a thriving business with a growing customer base.

BOOTSTRAPPING OR SMALL-SCALE STRATEGIES

Unless you've already grown a substantial business with a growing audience, it's important to start with small-scale, "bootstrapping" approaches. We recommend these strategies because you can use them with little up-front investment, and they'll start yielding results, one customer at a time.

Creating Case Studies from Interviews

Let's say you're just beginning to get your business going. Each new client and each dollar of revenue is a major milestone. At this early stage, the key is to maximize the potential for referrals from every single client. You can't do this in an automated, tech-driven way. The key is to reach out personally to each client you work with to schedule follow-up interviews. A natural time to do this is after someone completes a course or coaching program with you. And don't procrastinate! Reach out as soon as you can — while the course or program is fresh in your client's mind.

The first purpose of these interviews is to gather the feedback you need to build increasingly high-quality offerings over time. You're going deep into what is most effective for your customers (whether course participants, coaching clients, or other types of customers) and identifying what needs to be improved in their experience. You might learn, for example, that your coaching clients were feeling overwhelmed by the number of different exercises you asked them to complete in the middle of the program. Or that course participants loved your worksheets, but wanted more opportunities to ask you questions and get feedback.

At the same time, you'll also be gathering the foundational content for case studies, which are essential for getting referrals and for providing social proof. Case studies allow prospective clients to see that other people have worked with you, been successful, and achieved meaningful results. To get useful information for a case study, you'll need to prepare for the interview. First, get permission to record the audio and video of the interview. Then you'll walk through a series of questions, making sure to follow up by asking for clarification and additional detail as needed.

You structure your interview around these seven key questions:

1. What was the problem or concern you had that led you to consider this course/program?

2. What had you tried to solve this problem/concern before, if anything?

3. What was challenging about getting going with this topic or this approach?

4. What have been the results of this program for you, both tangible and intangible?

5. What was most surprising to you?

6. What are you most looking forward to next?

7. Any suggestions or tips for people who might be considering taking this course/program, or working with you as a client?

You'll then develop written and video case studies based on these interviews. Here's an example of how a video case study might be presented.

"It's totally worth undertaking the challenge."

Example Person

Life Coach And Psychotherapist, New York, USA

Example is a life coach and psychotherapist who helps stressed out and burnt out professionals find more peace and ease into today's challenging work environments. She had spent most of her career working one on one with people but she began to realize that wasn't sustainable. She wanted to move her business online, but …

This format presents a compelling headline, provides descriptive background and information about the client, and includes a brief video of her experience and success. (In this case, the video is about three minutes, but shorter or longer is OK too.)

Video is great, but it is not the only format. Longer written case studies can be powerful too. For example, organization coach Pam Woods presents engaging case studies on her website, describing the client, the situation, and how she helped. You can adapt this format by filling in these sections for each client case study:

- The Client
- The Situation
- What Was Done
- The Outcome

THE BUSINESS OF COURSES

Next, you can publish these case studies on your website or blog, and share them on social media. When you do so, invite the people profiled in the case studies to share them on their networks as well. This will help you reach many of their friends and colleagues, who might be potential clients.

Jump-Starting Referrals

These interviews aren't just about gathering information and creating case studies. They're also the perfect opportunity to begin seeding referrals. This requires a bit of fearlessness. You can start by asking a more specific question that can lead directly to referrals:

Candidly, was this course [or coaching program, etc.] good enough for you to enthusiastically recommend it to a good friend? If not, what are the areas that would need to improve to earn your recommendation?

You'll tailor your response based on how each person answers this question. If they're genuinely enthusiastic, you can segue naturally into asking for referrals. Simply ask, *"Do you know anyone who might be a great fit for this [course/coaching program/event]?"*

It's crucial to make it clear that you *want* referrals. I know this sounds absurdly obvious. Nevertheless, many people overlook the importance of having a clear intention to seek and earn high-quality referrals. Clients are unlikely to refer other people to you unless:

1. They trust you, they're genuinely satisfied with your service, and they're confident that a friend or colleague would also have a good experience with you.

2.   They know that you *want* and *can handle* referrals. This point is critical, because no one wants to waste a friend's time and attention by referring them to a service provider who isn't available to help them. If you've ever gotten a referral to a local building contractor who never returns your calls, you know how exasperating this can be.

So it's up to you to plant the seed. Make your intention explicit: *Yes, I do want referrals.* Communicate this intention with your tone and enthusiasm, and by asking specific questions. Then be patient. While it would be amazing if your client responded immediately, "Yes, I know John and Sally; I'll introduce you," that's rare. More likely you're putting the idea in your client's head, so when they talk to the right person in a few weeks or months, it pops up: "You should talk to Abe; he might be able to help!"

Neither creating case studies nor asking for referrals are big, scalable techniques that are going to blow up your business and get hundreds of people coming in right away. That's because at the bootstrapping phase, it isn't really possible to have that level of rapid growth — nor would you be ready to handle it! At this stage of your business, you should stay focused on getting the next client, and the next, and the next — then working to make each individual client delighted with their experience. Then they'll be glad to refer others to you.

Asking for Help

"If you don't ask, you won't get." It's a cliché for a reason: It's true. This applies in the context of asking for individual client referrals, as we

just discussed. But it applies equally when you're launching a new online course or program. As you plan your promotion, make time to email or call past participants and ask them to share your upcoming course on social media or with their personal network.

For example, say you ran a small-group coaching program last year with 12 participants. Take a few minutes to reach out to each person individually with a warm, personal email, text message, or phone call. Start by checking in on how they're doing, and how they've applied what they learned in your program. Then follow up to mention that you've got a new program (or a new session of your existing program) coming up, and you'd love it if they could share the details with anyone who might be interested.

Again, this likely won't yield dramatic results, and that's not the point — as you bootstrap your business to a meaningful level of revenue, each incremental client and course sign-up is extremely valuable.

GROWTH AND SCALING REFERRAL STRATEGIES

Now let's look at what to do if things are going well. Where should you start when you're ready to start growing referrals beyond these one-on-one personal strategies and word of mouth? In this phase of your business, you can consider implementing "viral" marketing strategies. These strategies attempt to amplify sharing via social loops — friends tell friends, who tell more friends, and so on.

Taking Advantage of Viral Sharing

One powerful approach is to offer a free challenge with a viral sign-up process. The challenge should be designed to bring people into your core offer. Of course, you'll need good content and engaging materials as part of the challenge, which may take time to develop. (In Chapter 9, we'll look at whether it makes sense to build this content yourself or acquire it.)

Let's start with an example, and then walk through how you can apply this model in your situation. As Ruzuku was gaining momentum a few years ago, we began hitting the limits of talking to individual customers and asking for referrals. So to continue growing our referrals, we designed a "30-Day Course Creation Challenge" as a free lead magnet program. While this program on its own was a great way to attract people to our services, it generated only occasional referrals.

To scale up its impact, we added a viral sharing component. We put together a set of desirable prizes, including a year's subscription to Ruzuku, a private coaching session with me, books on learning design, and so on. We then invited people to enter into a giveaway for these prizes by sharing the challenge with friends and on social media. The more referrals someone brought in, the better their chance at winning a prize.

To jump-start the social sharing loops, we promoted the challenge enthusiastically to our own mailing list and social media. As people signed up, they saw the opportunity to enter the giveaway, and many of them began to share the challenge with friends, and on their personal social media feeds. Thanks to this amplified sharing, we were able to enroll far more participants into the challenge than we could have only through our own promotion.

Here are the steps to apply this strategy for yourself:

1. Design a 5- to 30-day free challenge that leads into your core offering (such as a paid course or coaching program).

2. Provide an incentive for participants to share the challenge with friends; ideally, the incentive is strong enough that they share as widely as they can.

3. For the incentive, consider giving away prizes — such as free access to your program, free coaching, a book you love — that are compelling but don't require a big cash outlay.

4. Design the giveaway so that the more someone shares, the better their chances of winning. For example, if someone brings in 10 new leads (referrals), they should have more chances to win than someone who brings in only 2 new referrals.

5. Tracking referrals can be complex, so choose a tool that will make it easy to share and pick a winner. We've used UpViral successfully, but make sure to research and find a tool that fits your needs.

6. Set up your registration process so that as people sign up for the free challenge, they're encouraged to share it on social media.

Just to reiterate, because this is so important: Please keep in mind that this is a *scaling* strategy, not a "just getting started" strategy. This strategy is much more complex to set up and implement than conducting interviews and sending personal emails. Building the challenge itself takes time, although you can accelerate this by using off-the-shelf tools such as Ruzuku (to host the challenge) and UpViral (to manage social referrals), and by outsourcing some of the content development (which we'll explore further in Chapter 9). In other words, please don't be tempted to jump into this strategy if you're just beginning to get clients and revenue. The complexity will frustrate you, and you likely don't have enough reach with your mailing list and social media to generate significant results.

Additional Scaling Strategies

While creating viral referral campaigns is the biggest opportunity here, there are some smaller steps you can take that are also quite valuable for growing businesses.

MEASURE YOUR WORD OF MOUTH. You should be able to answer this question: How many referrals are you receiving each month, or for a particular offer? For example, if 20 people sign up for a new session of your course, how many were referred by friends and colleagues? Simply by measuring the number of referrals you're getting, you'll get insight into how well your referral processes are working, and whether the quality of your offers is consistently high enough to generate referrals. Moreover, by making it a habit to check on your referrals stats regularly, you'll be more likely to generate new ideas for encouraging referrals.

INTEGRATE SHARING INTO YOUR COURSES. When is someone most likely to want to share your course? To answer this question, consider an insight from Nobel Prize–winning psychologist Daniel Kahneman. His work on the "peak-end rule" found that our most intense memories of an experience come from the "peak" (the most intense moment) and the end of the experience. These are the moments of most complete engagement and energy — and that's exactly when you should encourage people to share your offerings. Consider adding information on how to share your course into the welcome email you send when someone signs up for your online program. Then design an activity at the end of the course to encourage people to send a link to friends or share it on social media.

PROVIDE SPECIAL REFERRAL OFFERS. Consider providing "bring a friend" offers or other special deals that clients can share with friends. While people love sharing valuable content and resources with friends, what they love even more is being able to give a friend a deal or discount! This could be as a simple as a "friends and family" coupon with a fixed discount. Or you might allow people to sign up with a partner at a special package price.

HOW JANE COULD ELICIT REFERRALS

Let's return to Jane's situation to see how this plays out in practice. Jane has a roster of past coaching clients, so she could start her referral work by reaching out to those clients, setting up interviews, and creating case studies. This is the simplest step to get started and will help her achieve her goal of getting more consistent client flow.

Once she has a solid set of case studies online, Jane could look into running a free challenge with viral sharing. For example, many of her clients want help identifying a direction and focus for their life and career. To serve that need, she could set up a five-day "Your Level 10 Life" challenge using the viral referral strategy laid out earlier. She'd design this challenge to lead into either a paid group coaching program, or into Discovery calls on which she'd offer a paid one-on-one coaching package.

APPLY IT

To define your strategy for growing referrals and word-of-mouth revenue, start by clarifying what stage you're at. Are you bootstrapping — getting your first few clients? Or are you growing steadily with an established client roster, and looking for ways to further scale your growth? Most people should start with conducting interviews, building case studies, and asking for referrals. Even if you're growing, it's powerful to have this foundation in place. Then, if your revenue is looking good and you're seeing the benefits of personal referrals begin to plateau, you can start investing your time in more scalable strategies, such as a viral challenge.

LOOKING AHEAD

We've covered a lot: You've mastered the five phases of your customer's learning journey and gained a deep understanding of how to grow your business with online courses. But so far, we've been side-stepping around the actual *development* of the courses that would fit into the different phases of the learning journey. So, in Part 3, we'll turn our attention to how you go about building an online course, and then deciding whether to build a course yourself or acquire professionally designed course assets.

PART III

WHAT IT TAKES TO BRING YOUR COURSE TO LIFE

CHAPTER 8

BUILDING AN ONLINE COURSE FROM THE GROUND UP

YOU'RE AT A CROSSROADS. If you design a great course, you create a bond with your customer, enjoy fantastic word of mouth, and unlock unlimited potential for a long-lasting relationship. But if you create a bad course, you could disappoint your client — and perhaps lose their interest, forever. The stakes couldn't be higher.

As a solopreneur or small-business owner, you're undoubtedly juggling multiple jobs. In the morning, you may be spending some time as the accountant, then put on your "marketing coordinator" hat. After lunch you're the social media manager, followed by running operations and managing projects after your coffee break. To launch an online course, you may need to add "course design wizard" to that job roster.

In this chapter, we'll walk through the critical steps necessary to build a successful online course, including:

- Determining the scope of the course
- Creating the core materials (written self-study content, presentation slides, discussion questions, etc.)
- Designing any supplementary materials (worksheets, coaching questions, etc.)

And that's just the course alone. You'll also need to market it skillfully and use it as a springboard to nurture a customer community.

It's a lot — but I'll guide you through the process so you have a clear road map to follow.

STEP ONE: FINDING YOUR SUBJECT

You have the sense that you *should* create a course. But where to begin? The first step is to explore what your course will cover. The topic of your course should be:

- A subject that you know well. You need to know what you're teaching inside and out.
- A subject that you have passion for! If you don't care, why should anyone else?
- A subject that your customers care about. No one wants to teach to an empty room.

With these three principles guiding you, you can create a course that is engrossing for you, makes for a compelling offer, and is both interesting and valuable for your participants. That's a win-win-win.

But there are so many topics you know well that it can be difficult to determine which one is course-worthy. This is where it can be helpful to examine your existing client base. What do your customers frequently ask about? What problems are your customers (or people very similar to your customers) seeking solutions for?

EXAMPLE

Scenario: Jessica is a yoga teacher, with a robust in-person practice. She's noticed an uptick in Instagram comments on her posts from people who aren't in her hometown and are looking for ways to de-stress during the workday.

Now that you have your subject matter in mind, let's move on to the next key question: the scope of your course offering. You'll define your scope by thinking through whom your course is for, what their needs and questions are, and how to focus your offering so it's accessible and useful (rather than overwhelming!) for your clients.

EXAMPLE

Jessica knows she wants a way to reach working professionals wherever they are, but that's a broad mandate. Based on that idea, she brainstormed many different ideas for courses, such as:

- Lunchtime yoga: A short yoga class made for a 30-minute lunch break.

- Ergonomic office assistance: The course could include ways to design your desk space to make you feel both comfortable and supported during the workday.

- Happy hour cooldown yoga: An online yoga class specifically designed to de-stress after work. Jessica could also include nonalcoholic cocktail recipes that emphasize health, like her patented green juice that she has for her in-studio experience.

- "Lean In" yoga: Mixing yoga practice and women's empowerment, Jessica could create a course that encourages women to get more out of the workplace, including talks from outside speakers on issues like pay parity and networking.

- Guided meditation vacation: Jessica could create a guided meditation that offers a "quick vacation" from your workday.

You get the idea — there are endless possibilities. Coming up with a topic can be surprisingly easy. Much harder is paring that topic down so it's focused, easy to sell, and effective for your clients. Looking at your customer base can be a great way to narrow the scope of your course. Ask yourself the following questions as you determine the length and breadth of the course you're creating:

- How much time do my customers have to spend going through a learning experience with me?

- Am I planning to offer a follow-up course?

- What "solution" do I want my course to provide for my customers?

- How does this course fit into my business model, and my Customer Learning Journey Model?

Your mission is to provide a course that is both informative and productive. Determining the correct scope for the project is essential to fulfilling both of these objectives. To make this concrete, let's take a look at how Jessica might answer these questions about her course scope:

EXAMPLE

How much time do Jessica's customers have?

- Jessica's customer base ranges in age from 25 to 45. The majority of her customers are female, work full-time, and are parents. They typically have 1–3 hours per week to devote to learning. This suggests that courses demanding many hours of work for multiple weeks or months may not fit into her customers' schedules. But a 30-minute lunchtime course is very doable for her customer base!

Is Jessica planning on offering a follow-up course?

- If Jessica's guided meditation and short yoga program is a hit, she plans on creating an online community space for yoga practitioners to connect and network. She hopes to apply the mindfulness of yoga to the stressful life of corporate America.

What "solution" does Jessica want to provide to her customers?

- Jessica wants both to create a space of community and to provide them with action-oriented solutions to common workplace issues like stress and aching eyes from continuous screen time.

What "solution" does Jessica want to provide for her business?

- Jessica sees the course as a way to expand her in-person business and build a dedicated online following. She also sees it as a stepping-stone to her ultimate goal, which is to create a space of community, both online and off.

By answering these simple questions, Jessica was able to pare down her broad vision of "office stress + yoga" to a specific, focused course. She'll provide a mini-course on mindfulness with a series of guided meditations and easy stretches. This course will address her customers' immediate needs, while opening the door for further classes and strengthening her revenue streams.

STEP TWO: STRUCTURING YOUR COURSE

The second step in your course-building process is *structuring* your course: crafting an effective step-by-step outline that leads your participants toward meaningful outcomes. Like the other aspects of designing an effective course, this can be surprisingly challenging.

My favorite way to start is open-ended exploration. Start with your high-level vision of why you want to offer a course, and how it could help your clients. Then let your imagination run wild. Give space for all the ideas bursting out of your brain. Take time to do this before attempting to wrangle your outline into a polished, cohesive whole. This is not the time to edit. This is a time to write freely, and let all ideas (from the amazing to the not-so-good) have their turn. I also find that the tactile element of using pen and paper (rather than a Word or Google document) reduces the tendency toward automatic editing. There's something about physical writing that makes the process more immersive.

Once your ideas have poured onto paper, it's time to begin editing. To start, create three columns:

- Beginning
- Middle
- End

Whether a two-hour intensive or a six-week workshop, a course needs to have a narrative structure, similar to your favorite nonfiction book or Netflix documentary. Consider the length of the course, and begin to separate your ideas accordingly. For example, if you're designing a six-week intensive course on embroidery, an entire class in the "middle" section of your course could be spent on how to set up good stitches for lettering. But if the course is a two-hour introductory experience, there won't be time to go as in-depth on those skills.

The sections of a course should flow naturally, from one to the next. In particular, if a concept or skill is necessary to understand or apply an idea at the end of the course, you'll need to teach it at the beginning. It's also important to keep a *minimalist* perspective in mind as you structure your course. Avoid including information that isn't necessary to help participants move toward the key goals of the program.

You might find it helpful to start editing your course outline in a digital tool. I like the outlining tool Workflowy, or consider any of the following tools for creating digital "boards" and "mind maps":

- Trello (trello.com)
- Asana (asana.com)
- Lucidchart (lucidchart.com)
- MindMeister (mindmeister.com)

All of these programs allow one to move items easily from one column or area to another. Prefer to keep the process tangible? Use Post-it notes or index cards taped to a wall or pinned on a corkboard.

You're beginning to firm up the "narrative" of your course. Once this narrative is set and all lessons are in their corresponding beginning/middle/end columns, it's time for the more detailed work of designing specific lessons. This may include breaking the beginning, middle, and end columns into smaller subcolumns. These will represent core lessons or modules in your course (i.e., Lesson 1, Lesson 2, etc.).

For each lesson, consider the three *W*s of why, when, and what:

- **Why** is this lesson important? Why do students need to understand this concept, or learn this skill?

- **What** specific steps or ideas need to be taught in this lesson? What key takeaways will this lesson lead to?

- **When** will students use this concept or technique? How long will it take them to learn this skill? How much practice will they need to integrate and apply the ideas in their life or work?

Remember that for an expert (that's you!), it can be easy to omit certain steps or information that are integral to the learning experience. For an experienced email marketer, creating a compelling email subject line is a matter of routine. But for someone brand-new to email campaigns, this step can take a very long time to learn and require hours of trial and error.

A good exercise is to imagine that you are explaining the core process and concepts in your course to a visitor from Mars (bear with me here!). If this alien visitor had never heard of anything being taught in your course — starting with the absolute basics — how would you go about explaining the core ideas? You'll find that you're forced to set aside assumptions, and break concepts down into small, easily understandable components. That's the key to creating effective explanations in your course.

Keep in mind that each course should have a clear, observable outcome for students. By the end of the course, students should have changed in some way: understood a new approach, mastered a specific technique, or shifted their behavior. Write down these ideal outcomes. These will be the North Star for your course design. If, by the end of the course, students are able to show significant progress toward the envisioned outcomes, then the course was a success.

To sum up, these are the key steps for structuring your course:

- **Brain dump:** Get all your ideas onto paper or into a digital document, without self-editing.

- **Craft a narrative:** Sequence key concepts into beginning, middle, and end.

- **Be an investigator**: Write out the why, what, and when of each lesson. Why is this lesson important? What do participants need to complete this lesson? When will these skills come into play?

- **Dive deep:** Break broad ideas into specific lessons. Craft an "ideal outcome" for each lesson.

- **Outline lessons:** Craft your key points for each lesson.

Now take a deep breath, because the trickiest steps in course design are yet to come.

STEP THREE: CREATING AND REVISING YOUR CONTENT

Grab your draft outline and a cup of coffee, because the time has finally come to create your content. First, gather background information to inform your content development. If you have a shelf full of relevant books, go through them and identify key ideas to use when writing. Maybe you've read articles online about your topic. Make a list of all the resources you can refer to when developing specific course materials. You don't want to lose anything you need during this process, so you might start creating an itemized list or spreadsheet to keep track of books, articles, presentations, and other resources.

You'll then begin preparing activities for both consumption (providing information) and interaction (requiring student participation). Following are some of the most common formats you can consider including in each category.

Informative learning activities

- **Written lessons:** Written materials (such as overviews, summaries, and step-by-step guides) are critical for learning because they require a different type of focus than audio or video presentations. Writing also enables learners to easily review a concept multiple times and integrate it into their own mental model.

- **Presentations or slideshows:** Slideshows (such as a PowerPoint or Keynote presentation) allow you to represent concepts visually, so you can bring them to life for your participants. Say you're teaching a specific principle of graphic design. You'll want to show this principle visually for your students on a slide. In addition to their value in delivering a live or on-demand presentation, your slideshows can also serve as a takeaway for students. They can download or print the slide deck to refer to, again and again.

- **Video:** While creating good videos can be complex, there's a payoff: connecting with your students on a visual and emotional level.

- **Audio:** Audio-only presentations can provide a key benefit of video — hearing your voice, tone, and energy — while taking much less time to produce. Audio is also a great format for participants who need to learn "on the go" — they can listen to lessons while walking or commuting, for example.

Interactive learning activities

- **Worksheets:** Worksheets can serve multiple purposes: summarizing valuable information for students, providing a takeaway item that they can download and print, and helping participants move from passive to active learning. Worksheets can be completed during a live webinar or group coaching session, or can be given as "homework" to be completed offline.

- **Discussion questions:** One of the most powerful ways to activate deeper learning is to have participants share their reflections and perspectives with you and with each other. You can facilitate this interaction by setting up specific discussion questions or prompts in an online course platform such as Ruzuku, or in a dedicated online community tool.

- **Quizzes:** Quizzes will help your participants self-assess their own knowledge, and also help you measure their progress. Are they really "getting" the key concepts in the way you anticipated? Are they on track toward the intended outcomes of the course? Will they walk away with a solid understanding of the material?

Seek both variety and balance in your selection of learning activities. The most engaging courses contain a diverse set of materials that both help your students learn new concepts and guide them to action.

Once you've gathered all of these resources and finalized the outlines for your lessons that you wrote in step two, it's time to start actually creating your course content. This includes writing lessons, designing worksheets, scripting and recording videos, and so on. We'll walk you through an example.

You may be wondering how long the content creation process will take. We recommend first starting with outlines. Then plan for the creation of each detailed lesson (whether written content, a video, etc.) to take a few hours. That could add up to several weeks of work if your course contains numerous modules with a range of learning activities. Make sure also to include editing and revision time in your estimates, because it can be substantial. For example, we recently developed a six-module course on goal-setting that took over two months to write, revise, and edit.

Whatever content you develop, it's important to build in a revision and editing process, which often entails getting fresh eyes on your final draft. When you have deep experience with your course topics, it's natural to gloss over explanations, or accidentally skip steps when creating your materials. So consider finding an editor who can help you gauge if your course materials are written at an accessible level. If you find that leads to some challenging feedback, don't give up! After all, people get master's degrees in instructional design for a reason: It's complex. Don't be surprised if you need to make substantial revisions to your initial draft to create a course that's effective, engaging, and accessible to your intended client.

For some inspiration, let's look at a sample lesson outline from Jessica's 30-minute "Lunch Break Mindfulness" course. This detailed lesson outline could then be adapted into a written summary, a live webinar, or an audio or video recording.

EXAMPLE

Greetings: Say hello! Introduce myself, and don't forget to say the name of my business. Tell the short story about how my business got started. Welcome everyone to "Lunch Break Mindfulness."

Introduction: How I got involved in yoga. Tell that story about how I struggled in the rat race, and how I wanted to create a space for professionals to come and be free of all outside pressures.

Why Stretching is Important: Pivot into explaining how an office workplace can contribute to poor health.

Part 1. Recognizing your strengths: Take a deep breath and recognize your strengths. Read a quote here about strength, and don't break into a complete guided meditation but do a quick series of mantras. Suggest that they write them down.

Part 2. Stretches: Go over the stretches that one can do to make the day in the office a little less painful. Go over some hamstring, arm, and wrist stretches. Do some neck stretches. Suggest the Pomodoro Technique as a good way to get you off your computer for some stretches of time.

Part 3. Guided Meditation: Once the stretches are done, do a guided meditation I specifically created for office stretch. Acknowledge that some of that stress is outside your control. End with the mantras from the top.

Place of Community: Tell the story about how I want to create a space — online and off — for people to reconnect with their bodies, themselves, and their space.

Recap: Give a brief rundown of everything we did. Tell them that the mantras from the top are available to print on my website, and that this mindfulness meditation is here for them whenever.

Goodbye: Send them home with a wave, and a final deep breath. Don't forget to plug my website!

Notice how Jessica draws on anecdotes from her own life, provides great tips on stretching while at work, and creates a sense of shared community. Your course doesn't have to look like Jessica's, but the principles are the same: Your course should feel like an interesting conversation, not a dry lecture. Think about how you can connect with your participants on a personal level, while also sharing valuable instruction.

STEP FOUR: CHOOSING A PLATFORM

The last step is to choose a platform to host your courses online. There are so many options today, it can be hard to know which one to pick. Plus, as the co-founder of a platform (Ruzuku) myself, I'm incredibly biased! So for this step, don't just take my word for it — do your research.

When sourcing a course platform, it's smart to go back to step one. Reflect on what kind of experience you want for your customers — and what capabilities you need for yourself — so your course will be successful. Use these success criteria to guide your selection of a course platform.

To help define those criteria for yourself, consider this checklist of common requirements:

- Set a schedule on which your course will run, so you can easily facilitate "cohorts" of learners and foster community.

- Manage a course calendar (including releasing lessons on certain dates, and scheduling live webinars at specific times).

- Monitor the progress of students so you can follow up and keep individual participants on track. These analytics can be a key element in grasping which parts of your courses connected with students and which components were less successful.

- Host the types of content you'd like to include in your course, such as text, video, audio, PDF, and so on.

- Provide rapid and easy course setup. If it takes you hours to upload the documents and videos each time you create a course, you're far less likely to develop new courses or update existing material.

- Offer a simple and engaging experience for your course participants. How hard will it be for your students to pay, join the course, and begin participating? If any of these steps are a hurdle, it could mean a much lower participation rate.

- Foster online community and discussion. Ideally, you want a course platform that enables you to create a sense of community among your learners. If there is nowhere on the platform for students to share ideas with one another, you're missing out on a key component, not just of learning but of growing your business.

- Provide training and support on how to make the most of the course platform. Is there a clear, step-by-step process for setting up a course? Is there a responsive customer service team both for you as the course creator and for your students?

It's important also to consider the technical know-how of your ideal course participant. If your course participants are young, tech-savvy digital natives, then you don't need to worry much about their ability to master your online course setup. But if your customer base is more tech-phobic, it's critical to choose a course platform that makes signing up and participating in your course as simple as possible. If your clients can't navigate your course, they won't get value out of it, and they certainly won't refer others to it!

Take a couple of days to research criteria and options for hosting your online course. During this time, you can whittle down your list of requirements and providers. There's no need to rush into this, because uploading your course content is a significant task on its own. While you can always switch platforms at a later date, that can be a pain. Ideally you'd like to get started on a platform you're comfortable with so that you don't need to shift directions midstream.

High-level exploratory research is valuable, but the ultimate test is to go hands-on. Start a trial account on each platform you're considering, and test it out with your success criteria at hand. Then test the responsiveness and helpfulness of customer support. If you have a question, or your student is having issues with logging in, what kind of assistance do you receive? Put each course platform you are considering through its paces before making a final decision.

If the course platform offers an easy way to gauge student interest and report feedback, even better! Getting this feedback straight from students, and having an easy place to store it inside your course platform, will help you as you engage in the process of updating course material.

One final tip: When you upload your content to your course platform, don't forget to save an extra just-for-you-copy on Google

Drive, Dropbox, or an external hard drive. Although you may not access this material very frequently, it is good to have a second copy in a safe place that you own, rather than one owned by your third-party course platform.

CONCLUSION

This chapter is meant as a brief guide in creating an online course. It's far from exhaustive — we'd need an entire book or multi-month training program to go into the full details of course creation. If you get overwhelmed during your own course creation process, or it takes longer than you expected, remember that there are people who specialize in instructional design and course development. Don't feel discouraged just because you thought building a course would take you a month and it winds up taking a year. This isn't at all unusual.

And once you've created the course? Don't get too attached. As you run the course and gather student feedback, you'll find holes you need to fill. Lessons that you thought were going to be winners turn out to be confusing or incomplete. You'll always need to update and change your lessons based on real-world usage, so don't be afraid to go back to the drawing board. Just remember to push through and, when necessary, give yourself breaks. Don't be afraid to put your course-making to the side for a week when things just aren't coming together.

Then, if you find yourself overwhelmed with the responsibility of course creation, bear in mind that there are alternatives. In the next chapter, we'll lay out the benefits and drawbacks of buying a course versus building one yourself.

CHAPTER 9
BUILD VERSUS BUY

OVER THE PAST FEW YEARS, I've been on a mission to connect with the global community of course creators. I've spoken with artists, lawyers, healers, coaches, fitness experts, authors, and many others — all seeking to create different types of online courses and programs. In addition to my own interviews, we've sent out feedback forms in our courses, and analyzed industry surveys of over 1,000 online entrepreneurs and course creators. Through this research, we've been able to identify the top challenges course creators face and propose solutions. So let's dive into the data.

The first key insight is that only a small percentage of people who *want* to build a course have actually done so. Specifically, in our most recent survey, 40.6% of respondents were thinking about building a course, and 38.8% were working on one. But only 16.9% have built one or more complete courses. In short, the vast majority of people — more than 80% — want to *have* a course to grow their business, but haven't been able to *build* one successfully (at least, not yet!).

We wanted to better understand why this is happening, so we further asked respondents about their biggest course-building challenges. Two key challenges stood out: "finding the time" (reported by 47.4% of people), and "setting up the technology" (reported by 33.5%). We saw quotes like these over and over again from people sharing their biggest challenges:

- "Finding the time to get this up and running"
- "Time to make it happen"
- "Time management in writing and marketing the course"

And this makes sense. As we saw in Chapter 8, there are several time-consuming steps needed to create a full-fledged course, including conducting research, doing instructional design, creating content, and developing marketing collateral. Plus, time is especially scarce if you're a coach, consultant, or other service provider. You're busy serving your clients, which doesn't leave too many hours in the day for research, content development, or copywriting.

So, that gives you two options: You can get better and faster at doing course development yourself. Or you can get help. And this can be hard! Whether consciously or not, many of us feel that we must be completely self-sufficient. We feel compelled to build everything ourselves. It's not easy to let that mindset go. Indeed, I've fallen into this trap myself — in reverse. For years people have asked me for help in building courses, and I was always skeptical of their requests.

"CAN YOU JUST BUILD THE WHOLE COURSE FOR ME?"

That's the question people have been asking me for several years. *I just don't have the bandwidth to do it myself. Can you help?* It's an understandable request; courses are powerful tools for creating the freedom, leverage, and impact that many independent experts seek, yet they're also challenging to create. We've always recommended, though, that people create their own courses from scratch. Sure, we provide easy-to-use technology and training to help make the process as painless and efficient as possible. But it's still up to you to plan the course, structure the outline, create the content, and develop the marketing materials. That process could take months.

And, having designed many courses myself, I understand the appeal of getting some help! I've been through the slog, sweating the details of module sequencing, script writing, and slide finagling. It's like the famous saying that countless writers, from Frank Norris to George R.R. Martin, have repeated versions of with resignation:

"I hate writing, but I love having written."

So I could imagine why people were so attracted by the promise of being able to skip all of that — to bypass all the research, content creation, tech setup, and marketing — and jump right to the fun part: having the course ready to go. That's why people kept asking me, "Can you just build the whole course for me?" And as exciting as that prospect is, many things make it challenging to have an entire course "done for you." That's why until very recently, my answer was always no — you *can't* outsource your entire course.

More recently, though, I've come to see a different point of view — one that's led me to change the advice I give. So what's changed? In short, it's exactly what we've reviewed in the past few chapters: There are many ways to use courses throughout your customer's journey. As you enhance each phase of the learning journey with courses, you reach more customers, serve them better, and earn more revenue. Yet at the same time, it's unrealistic for most independent experts to build courses to support all those scenarios. But if you *don't* have courses to augment your customer's learning journey, you're letting big opportunities slide right by.

In particular, many people tend to have a laser-like focus when it comes to courses: building a flagship program based on their own ideas and techniques, and making that their core revenue offering. That's the type of course you need to build entirely from scratch. And it's the kind of course that's been heavily hyped in the industry. But that form of course offering reflects just *one* phase of your customer's learning journey. And a "flagship" program isn't necessarily the best way to start with courses, especially if you're an early-stage business, focused on coaching, consulting, or other services. In that scenario, your priority should be building cash flow through direct service offerings. Your courses should focus on Discovery and Engagement — bringing potential clients into your orbit. These are also the types of courses that you can most effectively outsource, so you can get them up and running quickly.

To understand if outsourcing is right for you, it's important to understand two concepts: proprietary transformation and opportunity cost.

Proprietary Transformation

Consider two approaches to building a course. One approach is to design a course that's based on your own intellectual property, which you deploy to help your customers achieve some result or transformation. That's what we call the "proprietary transformation" approach to online course development. For example, perhaps you teach managers a unique way to motivate their team using neuroscience principles that you discovered in your own Ph.D. research. Because this is your own proprietary approach and techniques, you'll need to design and develop the course yourself.

But only a fraction of courses falls into this category. Often your clients are asking for help with common problems, and when a problem is common, there's typically a "best practice" solution available. Depending on the type of work you do, here's how this scenario might play out. If you're a consultant to local small businesses, you might find that they aren't very disciplined and consistent about setting annual and quarterly goals for their business. You can draw on best practices around setting and reviewing goals to help them be more effective. Or, if you're a wellness coach, you might find that many of your clients are getting poor sleep, which is affecting every other aspect of their health. There are common best practices around getting a good night's sleep, which you could provide to your clients to help them achieve rapid improvements.

These best practices aren't unique to you — and that's OK! Not every part of your business has to be unique, it just has to *work*: to provide meaningful results for your clients. This concept will make a lot more sense if we pause for a moment and talk about cinnamon rolls.

There are a couple of places you can get coffee and a cinnamon roll in my hometown of Carrboro, North Carolina. There's global giant Starbucks, famous around the world for its coffee, which also sells some pastries on the side (because they know many people will want a sweet bite with their coffee). And there's local hero Weaver Street Market, a small co-op grocery store that's famous (around these parts, at least) for delicious croissants, cinnamon rolls, and many other baked goods. Weaver Street Market's rolls *have* to be delicious — their reputation is what brings people into the store. Starbucks' strategy is to lure people in with fancy coffee drinks, and just sell a few pastries on the side (and the pastries themselves don't have to be spectacular).

So, who makes the rolls at each store? Weaver Street Market has their own in-house recipes and proprietary bakery (the Food House, down the road in Hillsborough). Starbucks, instead, sources their rolls from a contract bakery somewhere in the region. Pastries aren't their core offering, so they strategically outsource the development of these products to a more specialized producer. This works in each case, because the strategies are different. For Weaver Street Market, the strategy is to be known for unique, proprietary, and delicious pastries, so they invest in the in-house development. For Starbucks, the strategy is to *complement* world-class coffee drinks with a few pastries that meet customer's demand for a sweet snack.

The same distinction — *core* versus *complementary* — applies with courses. For a course that is *core* to the transformation and techniques you offer to people, it's important to build it yourself with your own proprietary approach. For courses that are part of the rest of your customer journey — helping people discover you, nurturing them to a sale, and retaining them over time — you don't necessarily need to do all that heavy lifting.

So here's the question: Do you want to have *only* a core transformation course for business? Only noncore, complementary courses? Or both? When we've surveyed people who participate in our bootcamps, the vast majority answer either (a) noncore, or (b) both. Very few want only a core transformation course. If that resonates for you, you can see why it may make sense to look at outsourcing development of your noncore courses, just like Starbucks does with their cinnamon rolls.

Opportunity Cost

Why is it important to consider strategic outsourcing? Why does Starbucks, which could surely invest in baking its own scones and croissants if it wanted to, rely on contract bakeries instead? The answer lies in a concept you might recall from a dusty copy of your *Economics 101* textbook: opportunity cost. According to economist David R. Henderson:

> When economists refer to the "opportunity cost" of a resource, they mean the value of the next-highest-valued alternative use of that resource. If, for example, you spend time and money going to a movie, you cannot spend that time at home reading a book, and you cannot spend the money on something else. If your next-best alternative to seeing the movie is reading the book, then the opportunity

cost of seeing the movie is the money spent plus the pleasure you forgo by not reading the book.

Any initiative that you invest time and money in has an opportunity cost. Starbucks *could* develop its own recipes, build bakery facilities, hire staff, source ingredients, and so on. But their executives recognize that these investments come with an opportunity cost. They prefer to invest the time and money in other projects that are more rewarding — perhaps developing new coffee drinks, rolling out marketing campaigns, or improving their mobile app. You can apply this same analytical lens to your course-building initiatives.

As we've discussed, building a high-quality course is hard and time-consuming. This means creating your own course from scratch has a large opportunity cost: You could be investing that time and effort on other areas of your business, such as serving clients, improving your marketing channels, writing a book, and so on. For many individual experts, it's a challenge to carve out the time from your client commitments to build a course. On top of that, you face the conundrum of figuring out the technology for course setup and delivery. So what to do? One approach would be to save time by throwing money at the problem. You could hire specialized experts to design the course outline, create engaging content, and set everything up on a modern course platform.

But even if it makes sense in theory to outsource in this way, you have to consider the price tag of hiring someone else, or perhaps even multiple "someone elses." You might need each of the roles shown here, which could mean you're looking at spending in the range of $5,000–$50,000 in hard (direct payments) and soft (your own time) costs, especially if you've never created a course before and are figuring it out for the first time.

That's not a feasible investment for most people. So what's the alternative?

The Power of Integrated Outsourcing

One option is to license pure content. Traditionally, this was the realm of "PLR" (private label rights) providers. A number of companies have offered "done for you" content such as e-books, articles, webinar slides, and so on. You can license these materials for your own work in different areas to save time.

Unfortunately, this type of content fails to fully address the needs of contemporary experts who are seeking to serve their customer's journey with engaging and modern online courses. What's needed, first and foremost, is to have courses developed for you and *implemented* on an easy-to-use technology platform. Otherwise, you're back to square one of having to choose and set up tech yourself, which is a huge barrier for most people. In addition, effective courses aren't just about "content." They need to be carefully structured to avoid overwhelm, and to encourage participants to take action. Dumping content that was intended for an e-book, blog post, or report into a course will likely lead to a course that is less than satisfactory for participants and results in a disappointing impact for your business.

What's really needed is an integrated solution. Integrated outsourcing of online courses can address all four of the challenges you face:

1. Finding enough time to create a high-quality course
2. Choosing and configuring modern course-hosting technology
3. Providing a wide range of course topics to address the different ways you could serve customers throughout their learning journey with you
4. Developing persuasive marketing materials, including offer pages and email campaigns

This integrated outsourcing approach, by the way, is the exact philosophy we follow in our own work. If you're interested in learning more, check out our course catalog at http://instant.courses.

SEE JANE BUILD

A powerful insight is available to us in Jane's example. As we reviewed earlier, Jane is a professional coach, specializing in career coaching, but she also helps people with broader life goals and supports them in designing a life and career they love. Her initial revenue comes from private coaching clients, although she's also offered a handful of in-person workshops from time to time. She's in the dollars-for-hours model — she's only getting paid when her calendar is full. Jane has big goals for her business, including:

- Bring in coaching clients more consistently.
- Diversify her revenue so she's less dependent on feast-or-famine coaching.
- Better leverage her time.

We've already seen how Jane can use courses to enhance her customer's learning journey so she can achieve these big goals. Now let's apply this model to your situation. The question then becomes: Should you *build* the course content to support your business strategy yourself, or look to *buy* course materials and customize them for your needs?

In the next — and final — chapter, we'll help you put together all the ideas we've discussed. You'll see how to create a strategy and identify where to focus your efforts so you can start getting results with online courses.

CHAPTER 10
YOUR NEXT STEPS

MICHAEL PORTER, one of the world's leading experts on strategy, has a key insight that every business owner should take to heart: "The essence of strategy is choosing what not to do."

Before you put this book down (or turn off your Kindle), I'd like to help you to develop a clear idea of where to go from here — what to do, and what *not* to do. You should wrap up with a clear sense of where to focus your efforts so you can start getting results with online courses: in short, your *strategy*.

YOUR COURSE BUSINESS STRATEGY

Strategy is about making choices and accepting trade-offs. Both are difficult! So keep in mind that developing an effective strategy for using courses isn't a simple, quick fix. What's more, your answers will evolve over time. Let's start by thinking through a few key questions. You'll likely gain some immediate insights, but make sure to reflect on these questions regularly — your perspective and answers will change over time along with your business model, client base, and other factors.

What are your current offerings (coaching, consulting, services, workshops, etc.)?

To begin, consider the current scope of your business. What do you currently offer to your clients? The list might include one-on-one private coaching, consulting engagements, in-person or virtual workshops, other services, and even physical products (such as a workbook, journal, or planner). It's important to map these out first so you can consider how to use courses to complement and grow your existing offerings.

What do you want to improve in your business over the next 12 months?

Multiple ideas may come to mind here, and there's no need to censor your thinking. Just jot down everything that comes to mind, whether you want to have more time open on your calendar, take home more income, or work on new projects.

What's your overarching goal for the next 12 months?

You can focus your efforts by distilling these many possible ideas down to one big goal. Ideally, if you can make progress on this key objective, good things will happen elsewhere, too. Examples might include:

- Get a consistent flow of high-end coaching clients.
- Add an additional income stream without teaching in person.
- Leverage your time by working with groups instead of just one-on-one.

How can adding courses help you achieve that outcome?

Walk through each of the five phases of your customer's learning journey. For each phase, reflect on opportunities you see to improve how you serve your clients in that particular phase. For example, you might observe in the Engagement phase that you're not currently providing much education to help nurture people who are new to your work. So you could consider adding a free introductory course to better engage new prospects and lead them into your coaching offerings.

What is the biggest bottleneck between where you are now and achieving that desired outcome?

Think about what's standing between you and your overarching goal. When you think about your goal, what's the "but" that's holding you back? Your answer will help you identify where to focus your initial efforts. Some examples:

- You want to have consistent flow of clients every month, *but* you're not getting enough inquiries.
- You want to leverage your time better, *but* you lack clarity on what online course to offer.
- You've talked to clients and there's interest in signing up for a group program, *but* you haven't developed the structure and materials to support an online experience.

Where should you focus first?

Pick one priority to focus on initially so you aren't spreading yourself too thin. Generally, this should be the opportunity that will generate the most revenue. In some cases — particularly if your revenue is already strong — it might instead make sense to focus on making better use of your time.

What's the next step to move forward on that area of focus?

The key to getting projects moving, as productivity guru David Allen has explained, is to write down a crystal-clear next step. Be sure to identify the very next action you'll complete to advance the project toward success. Take a moment to determine what that action is for you. For example, let's say your priority is to develop the materials for an online group coaching program. Your next step might be to review your client notes and summarize the biggest needs that your clients have so you can address them in the program.

REVISITING JANE'S STRATEGY

Earlier, I presented a possible strategy for Jane, our example of a career coach who wants to grow her business and better leverage her time. Now we're in a position to see where her strategy came from! Let's review how the key course business strategy questions informed Jane's options.

What are her current offerings (coaching, consulting, services, workshops, etc.)?

Currently, Jane's revenue comes primarily from private coaching clients, although she's also offered a handful of in-person workshops from time to time. These were decently successful, bringing some additional revenue, but not a huge amount. This means she's living in the world of "dollars for hours" — she's only getting paid when her calendar is full of client appointments.

What does she want to improve in her business over the next 12 months?

Jane feels fortunate to have an established coaching business, but she'd like more flexibility and income than she has today. These are her goals:

- **Bring in coaching clients more consistently.** If it's November, she doesn't want to be stressed out, worrying, "Am I going to have enough clients coming in December and January to pay the bills?" She wants to have confidence that her pipeline of clients will generally be full.

- **Diversify her revenue so she's less dependent on feast-or-famine coaching.** When coaching is good, it's good — but then her calendar is maxed out. When the phone just isn't ringing with new client inquiries, she feels like she's spinning her wheels, unable to generate revenue with her free time. She wants to be able to earn money even when she's not super-busy with individual coaching clients.

- **Start better leveraging her time.** As Jane has gained experience and a strong reputation for her private coaching, she's seen more and more opportunity to expand beyond the "dollars for hours" model. She'd like to find ways to use online programs and group coaching to leverage her expertise.

What's her overarching goal for the next 12 months?

Fundamentally, Jane wants consistent, diversified revenue.

How can adding courses help her achieve that outcome?

There are three approaches Jane could explore to add courses (or the related modality of online group coaching) to her business.

STRATEGY 1: A FREE "LEAD MAGNET" MINI-COURSE

Jane could start by creating a free mini-course that aligns with the type of clients she wants to attract and work with. To kick-start the Discovery phase of her customer's learning journey, she'd share the mini-course consistently through her personal network and social media with a goal of enrolling at least 10 people per month and booking Discovery calls with at least two or three of those participants. In these Discovery calls, she'd explore people's goals, and then offer to enroll them into a coaching program if it seems like a good fit. This strategy would help her achieve her goal of having a consistent flow of coaching clients.

STRATEGY 2: A SMALL-GROUP LEVERAGED COACHING PROGRAM

To begin diversifying her revenue and leveraging her time, Jane could develop a group coaching program focused on goal-setting (a common need for her clients). By combining structured content with online discussions and small-group calls, Jane could create an engaging experience for participants, while serving more people than in a private one-on-one engagement. She'd set up this program on an online platform so it's easy for her to manage and for her participants to access. She might start by promoting this program twice a year, with a goal of $5,000 in revenue per promotion (say, 10 sign-ups @ $500 per person).

STRATEGY 3: THEMED QUARTERLY WORKSHOPS

Not all of Jane's prospective clients are immediately ready for the time commitment of a multi-week private or group coaching program. To better serve them, Jane could offer themed quarterly workshops, with follow-up exercises and discussions available in an online program for participants. Not only would the workshops generate revenue directly, but they would also be a great opportunity to invite participants into coaching packages via follow-up calls. Participants who experienced Jane's teaching in the workshops would be primed to consider the value of coaching. This strategy would both diversify revenue and contribute to consistent client enrollments.

What is the biggest bottleneck between where she is now and achieving that desired outcome?

Jane's biggest bottleneck is creating high-quality materials that would allow her to roll out the mini-course (for client acquisition) and leveraged offerings (the small-group program and workshops that rely heavily on content, worksheets, and discussion questions).

Where should she focus first?

Jane should focus on creating or acquiring the content she needs.

What's the next step to move forward on that area of focus?

She can research available options for sourcing the content she needs, including designing it herself, hiring a consultant, or licensing content from a high-quality provider. Then she can decide which approach to pursue, and how much to invest.

APPLY IT

Now it's your turn. Walk through each of the core strategy questions to define your focus and next steps.

- What are your current offerings (coaching, consulting, services, workshops, etc.)?
- What do you want to improve in your business over the next 12 months?
- What's your overarching goal for the next 12 months?
- How can adding courses help you achieve that outcome?
- What is the biggest bottleneck between where you are now and achieving that desired outcome?
- Where should you focus first?
- What's the next step to move forward on that area of focus?

TO BUILD OR TO BUY?

Whatever strategy you pursue, you'll likely need lots of high-quality course content. That raises the question we explored in Chapter 9: Should you build all your online course materials yourself, or look to acquire them from a trusted provider?

As we saw in Chapter 8, building a high-quality course can be both challenging (it requires a diversity of skills, from learning design to writing to visual layout) and time-intensive. So designing your own course entirely from scratch entails a significant opportunity cost. You could invest that time instead into other areas of your business: serving clients, developing a new keynote speech, writing blog articles, hosting a podcast, and so on. Because of this opportunity cost, many solopreneurs consider hiring specialized experts to design the course outline, create engaging content, and set everything up on a modern course platform. Unfortunately, this approach turns out to be prohibitively expensive for most early-stage businesses.

An alternative is to license just the content you need for a particular course. You may have seen, for example, PLR (private label rights) providers. A number of companies have offered "done for you" content such as e-books, articles, webinar slides, and so on. PLR content, however, generally doesn't meet the needs of contemporary experts who are seeking to serve their customers' journeys with engaging and modern online courses. You'll need courses that are set up on an easy-to-use technology platform. In addition, effective courses are much more than just "content." They're thoughtfully designed to avoid overwhelm. They invite participants to take action. So just shoehorning content that was intended for an e-book, blog post, or report into a course generally fails. It leads to an unsatisfactory course that has little business impact.

So if you decide to pursue the strategy of "buying" online courses for your business, it's important to look for an integrated solution. Integrated outsourcing of online courses can address all four of the challenges you face:

1. Finding enough time to create a high-quality course
2. Choosing and configuring modern course hosting technology
3. Providing a wide range of course topics to address the different ways you could serve customers throughout their learning journey with you
4. Developing persuasive marketing materials, including offer pages and email campaigns

This is the approach we take with our own products in our "Instant Courses" library. If you're interested in learning more, check out our course catalog at http://instant.courses.

WHERE DO YOU GO FROM HERE?

As we close, I have a final pep talk for you: Whatever you do, don't let technology get in the way of serving your learners. Make technology your ally, rather than something to fear. Recall Debra's story, which opened this book. Debra wasn't a technology guru, nor a master of complex business strategy. She was simply a passionate teacher and coach who was determined to both conquer her own burnout and serve her clients more effectively. That dual mission drove her to set up a Ruzuku account, license high-quality content, and then to customize and launch a series of successful online courses. If you're a coach or consultant like Debra, that means you can do it too. Like you, Debra didn't have any special tech background or knowledge, she'd never used a platform such as Ruzuku before, and she wasn't sure how to create or source her content. She just took the first step and figured it out as she went along. So that's my invitation to you. Be like Debra. Take the first step. After all, as Michael Altshuler has said:

"The bad news is time flies. The good news is you're the pilot."

ACKNOWLEDGMENTS

COUNTLESS THANKS TO:

Danny Iny for inspiring this book, and for pushing my thinking about online courses in new directions.

The amazing Ruzuku team, for building a product that helps course creators bring the ideas in this book to life.

The Mirasee team and community of students, for asking great questions and helping me clarify my ideas.

My family, for putting up with me staring at the MacBook more than is healthy, and doing a great job of feigning interest in online course development.

LETTER TO READERS

THANK YOU SO MUCH for picking up this book. I hope it helps you make online courses an integral part of your business, and I wish you great success.

If I can help in any way, please don't hesitate to get in touch. I love hearing questions from readers! My direct email is abe@ruzuku.com.

If you found this book useful, I'd so greatly appreciate a quick review on Amazon. Each and every review helps the book find new readers through Amazon's recommendations, so a few words from you can really make a difference.

Thanks, again!

Abe Crystal
Carrboro, North Carolina

ABOUT THE AUTHOR

ABE CRYSTAL, Ph.D., is the co-founder and CEO of Ruzuku, an online course platform focused on student engagement, as well as an adjunct professor in the School of Education at the University of North Carolina at Chapel Hill. He is an advisor to Mirasee, the online business education company, and helps guide their strategy for innovative online learning. Abe specializes in learning design and user experience research, and earned his Ph.D. in human-computer interaction at UNC-Chapel Hill.